ORTHO'S All About

Patios

Meredith® Books
Des Moines, Iowa

Ortho® Books
An imprint of Meredith® Books

Ortho's All About Patios
Editor: Larry Erickson
Art Director: Tom Wegner
Copy Chief: Catherine Hamrick
Copy and Production Editor: Terri Fredrickson
Contributing Writer: Martin Miller
Contributing Copy Editor: Steve Hallam
Technical Reviewer: John Riha
Contributing Proofreaders: Kathy Eastman,
    Margaret Smith, Julie Sunne
Indexer: Donald Glassman
Electronic Production Coordinator: Paula Forest
Editorial and Design Assistants: Kathleen Stevens,
    Karen Schirm
Contributing Editorial Assistant: Colleen Johnson
Production Director: Douglas M. Johnston
Book Production Managers: Pam Kvitne,
    Marjorie J. Schenkelberg

**Additional Editorial Contributions from
    Art Rep Services**
Director: Chip Nadeau
Designer: lk Design
Photo Editor: Nancy South
Writer: Clayton Bennett
Illustrators: Shawn Wallace, John Teisberg

Meredith® Books
Editor in Chief: James D. Blume
Design Director: Matt Strelecki
Managing Editor: Gregory H. Kayko

Director, Sales & Marketing, Retail: Michael A. Peterson
Director, Sales & Marketing, Special Markets:
    Rita McMullen
Director, Sales & Marketing, Home & Garden Center
    Channel: Ray Wolf
Director, Operations: George A. Susral

Vice President, General Manager: Jamie L. Martin

Meredith Publishing Group
President, Publishing Group: Christopher M. Little
Vice President, Consumer Marketing & Development:
    Hal Oringer

Meredith Corporation
Chairman and Chief Executive Officer: William T. Kerr

Chairman of the Executive Committee: E.T. Meredith III

Photographers
(Photographers credited may retain copyright ©
    to the listed photographs.)
William D. Adams: 10 (top)
Bob Braun: 6, 8 (TL), 11
Pat Bruno/Positive Images: 27
Karen Bussolini/Positive Images: 36 (top)
Grace Davies: 42, 43
Sue Hartley: 7 (center), 24 (top)
Shelley Hawes/Decisive Moment Photography: 21 (right),
    23 (right), 25 (right), 29 (right)
Jerry Howard/Positive Images: 7 (top), 20 (top), 86
Charles Mann: 8 (TR), 10 (bottom), 12 (bottom), 34, 35
Ann Reilly/Positive Images: 90
Jay Schug: 19 (bottom)
The Studio Central: 20, 21 (bottom), 22, 23, 24, 25 (bottom),
    26 (bottom), 28, 29 (bottom), 30, 31 (bottom), 32, 33 (top)
Deidra Walpole Photography: 9, 36 (bottom), 37

All of us at Ortho® Books are dedicated to providing you
with the information and ideas you need to enhance your
home and garden. We welcome your comments and
suggestions about this book. Write to us at:
    Meredith Corporation
    Ortho Books
    1716 Locust St.
    Des Moines, IA 50309–3023

If you would like more information on other Ortho
products, call 800-225-2883 or visit us at www.ortho.com

Note to the Readers: Due to differing conditions, tools,
and individual skills, Meredith Corporation assumes no
responsibility for any damages, injuries suffered, or losses
incurred as a result of following the information published
in this book. Before beginning any project, review the
instructions carefully, and if any doubts or questions remain,
consult local experts or authorities. Because codes and
regulations vary greatly, you always should check with
authorities to ensure that your project complies with all
applicable local codes and regulations. Always read and
observe all of the safety precautions provided by
manufacturers of any tools, equipment, or supplies,
and follow all accepted safety procedures.

SETTING YOUR GOALS 6

CHOOSING MATERIALS 16

REFINING THE DETAILS 34

PUTTING IT TOGETHER 42

SETTING YOUR GOALS

Whether you plan to use your patio for family dining, entertainment, recreation, or quiet contemplation, you'll enjoy it even more when you create it with your specific needs in mind.

If you're unsure of your overall goals, don't start shopping yet. And as tempting as it is to dive into digging and building, keep your toolbox closed long enough to think the project through. Consider how you want your patio to function, how you want it to look and feel, how it will work with your home and garden, and what kinds of weather and surface conditions will affect its comfort, appearance, accessibility, and durability.

You'll want to enjoy this outdoor addition to your home for many years, so the time you take now to plan carefully will save you from second-guessing and costly remodeling later.

Many patio designs are attractive, but not all of them will be right for you. Start with one question: What will make you want to spend time on it? Then build on that.

ELEMENTARY CHOICES

When planning your patio, take advantage of the variety of materials and their styles, shapes, colors, and patterns to create an outdoor living space that enhances your lifestyle and environment.

This book provides you with illustrated instructions that show how to construct the right patio for your home—as well as detailed information about the range of paving options—brick, concrete, flagstone, tile, wood, and gravel—that will express your style.

Remember that a patio is more than just a flat finished surface. It will include other elements—trees, gardens, fences, walls, steps, grills, furniture, and lighting—that are useful and attractive.

This inviting patio gains a sense of tranquillity from its natural materials and gentle shapes. A break in the flagstone surface creates a dramatic creek bed.

Contoured edging flows around trees and shrubs. Flowers at the edges add a gardener's touch, and the paved surface is smooth and level—useful in any season.

WHAT DO YOU WANT FROM YOUR PATIO ?

Patios extend your house into the outside world. Here, the brick pattern flows smoothly from the family room into the patio, creating a unified and natural extension of the indoor space.

Most patios serve multiple purposes for members of your family, for guests, and for different occasions. Take time to consider your lifestyle. Get the whole family together for a freewheeling discussion about how everyone wants to use and enjoy your new outdoor room. Make a wish list by category, and be prepared to make compromises. Start with a list of things you absolutely have to have and then add elements that are desirable but not required. Here are some things you should consider.

A GETAWAY

Even if your needs are simple—such as a place to enjoy the morning newspaper and a cup of coffee—you'll need comfortable seating. If your patio will be used primarily for family gatherings, the space doesn't need to be very large, but you'll want enough seating and table space to accommodate everyone. And if family dining is in your design, you'll also want a grill.

ENTERTAINING

Parties eat up patio space like guacamole dip—there's never enough. When friends drop by, patios and kitchens tend to fill up quickly. So if you entertain often, consider guests in your patio plans. Small groups may not require much more space or furnishings than a family would need; but for large gatherings, boost your patio's seating, cooking, and dining areas. Remember your teenagers: An outside patio offers them privacy and rewards you with peace in your home.

PATIOS ADD VALUE

A well-designed patio will add to the value of your home—you're actually adding to its livable square footage. Plan with care and buy the best materials you can afford—it's a sound investment.

CHILDREN'S PLAY SPACE

Patios can be perfect for children's play. Plan for children's ages as well as their number. If your yard is the neighborhood attraction, add the neighbor kids to your head count. Sandboxes are great adjuncts to patio space for families with toddlers. But if the kids are about to outgrow the sandbox, plan for the future. Tree forts, swings, and things to climb on are popular through the preteen years. A basketball court for older children might be better on the driveway, and weekend soccer can be played in the yard.

GARDENING

Consider the family gardener, and be realistic about how serious you are. Flowers and shrubs at the edging or raised beds add wonderful accents to a patio plan, but they require maintenance. Even if you're an enthusiast, keep your planting simple.

This patio takes advantage of existing shade, and the screened lanai offers an outdoor respite in rainy weather.

This airy setting, open to sunlight and breezes, offers a place to relax and also is just the right size for larger gatherings.

ACCESS

You'll enjoy your patio more—and more often—if it is conveniently located. A family room connection might be most common, but it isn't universally best. A small patio for coffee and the morning paper, for example, may be more convenient if it's adjacent to your bedroom or the kitchen. But the same sites would be disasters for party traffic. For privacy, look for ways to limit access— shielding your patio behind hedges or fencing, for example. For entertaining, look for ways to increase access, with doorways from rooms where you would entertain guests and with walkways that guide guests to and from your patio without traipsing through the house.

This quiet setting is flexible enough for many uses. Movable furniture and flower pots allow a fresh look for every season.

THE LOOK AND FEEL OF YOUR PATIO IDEAL

In settings with few trees overhead, or with broad surrounding views, create a subtle oasis of comfort by adding landscape elements that blend in with the scenery.

Formal and informal design elements combine to make this hideaway for two a more comfortable place to enjoy. Natural foliage and flowers soften a stark wall and contrast nicely with the nouveau-style furniture.

Your patio needs to be practical, of course, but don't stop there. You'll enjoy it and use it more when its style appeals to you and reflects your personality. An easy way to discover your own personal style is to take a tour of the neighborhood and make mental notes of things you like. Clipping photos and diagrams from magazines also is helpful. Whatever method you use, keep these points in mind.

FORMALITY

Style can be broken down into two broad categories, characterized by the use of lines, shapes, angles, and materials.
■ Formal patio designs feature straight lines, right angles, and regular geometric shapes. A formal layout might have a paved central circle surrounded by rectangular planting beds. Formal designs are symmetrical: If you imagine a line down the center, one side is a mirror image of the other.
■ Informal patio designs are marked by curved lines and irregular, often free-flowing, shapes. Balance and informality are the goals, rather than symmetry. Informal layouts typically use loose material—small stones, or wood chips—for surfaces, but many successful informal patios have brick in curving layouts. Informal patio designs often interweave gardens with paved patio areas.

HERITAGE

Style can be further categorized as traditional or contemporary.
■ A traditional patio evokes a feeling of the courtyard, and uses decorative items such as urns, fountains, columns, and lush foliage. Traditional patios usually incorporate formal lines, but can be found in informal designs as well. For example, you'd find steps built with brick in clean orderly edges in a traditional formal garden. In an informal traditional setting, the steps might be made of dry stacked stone.
■ Contemporary patios are cool, serene, and comfortable. A contemporary patio probably would include bolder shapes and colors, sleeker lines, and unusual combinations of materials, such as poured concrete inset with colorful tile. Decorative items are sleek and modern, with emphasis on color, texture, and light.

REGIONAL FLAVORS

Patio styles have evolved in many ways in different parts of the country due to climate, culture, and native plants and materials. It makes good sense to adopt regional aspects in the design of your patio because local plants and building materials are easier to find and less expensive. Also, regional styles make a good fit with your surroundings, and native plants will require less care and maintenance

than imports. However, don't restrict yourself dogmatically to your region. Bring in unusual ideas from distant places, especially those that won't require extra cost and maintenance. Include potted plants you can move indoors—they'll work miracles. A bonsai in a simple setting will help give your patio the look of a Japanese garden. Adobe pavers and cacti will create a Southwestern feel in a Midwest climate.

HARMONY

You don't need to be a slave to stylistic categories. Combine classic and modern styles to create a patio that has old-style charm and modern convenience. Harmony is the key to good design. No matter what style you choose, try to create a harmonious interaction among the different elements of your patio. Your outdoor living space should feel as if it complements your house. All the elements will look like they belong together. Use the following guidelines to help you harmonize your patio, home, and garden.

UNITY AND CONTRAST: Create a sense of continuity between your house and patio by using similar materials, colors, shapes, and textures in both. Use small, carefully placed patio elements to contrast color, shape, or texture. Gardens, edgings, walls, colored concrete, stone, tiles, bricks, logs, gates,

furnishings, lights, and decorative pieces— all add pleasing and lively accents.

Interweave trees and plants with your patio, or formally contain them on the perimeter with edging, fences, hedges, or planters. Don't crowd the paved areas—paving is for people.

As you consider various plants, think about how their textures, shapes, colors, and mature size will complement your structural materials.

HOW LARGE? A small patio can be overwhelmed by a huge house, and a lavish patio can seem out of proportion with a modestly sized home. As a rule of thumb, start with a design that is about a third of the interior area of your home, and adjust it until the scale suits your sense of proportion.

CENTER STAGE: Arrange walls, plants, and walkways so that they lead to a focal point— any object or view you want to call attention to. Place your main patio furniture around this area to give it greater definition.

If your patio is large or is made up of many smaller paved and garden areas, position smaller groupings of furnishings and decorative elements in ways that won't clutter your central area.

How will you know when the design you've created is harmonious?

It will look soothing rather than jarring. It will present a cohesive blend more than a jumbled clutter of parts, and its general impression will be inviting and comfortable.

Mix materials to create your own look. This patio forms a whimsical spiral with a combination of tile, brick, and concrete with aggregate. The extra time required to design and build a unique patio can clearly be time well spent.

THE LOOK AND FEEL OF YOUR PATIO IDEAL
continued

The backdrop of vines and the gentle curve of plantings soften the corners of existing walls in this comfortable, formal courtyard.

Once you have settled on a basic style for your patio, take a look at your site. There are things you may not have noticed that will affect not only how your patio will look, but also where you put it.

The configuration of your house will suggest certain shapes and locations for your patio.

ATTACHED: The typical attached patio is located next to the house, with immediate access to the interior—usually the kitchen or family room. In a U- or an L-shape house, you can take advantage of adjoining walls, but the contour of your patio doesn't have to be rectangular. Round the corners, create flowing patterns with your paving, and add shrubs to soften the corners.

WRAPAROUND: This is for the family that wants patio access from several rooms. A wraparound patio offers opportunity for multiple uses in a single patio—a quiet retreat outside the master bedroom, family dining off the kitchen, and parties that flow from the family room. Curved corners, garden beds, planter boxes, and low walls—independently or in combinations—will separate each area and give each its own character.

DETACHED: A detached patio is an excellent solution for sun and shade problems. Move the patio out from the house and into the natural surroundings to take advantage of existing trees and varied shade patterns. Connect the patio with a walkway that

This patio subtly combines organic and formal features, along with both traditional and contemporary elements.

A design doesn't have to be complicated to be interesting. As this patio shows, a brick pattern that stays consistent over the entire surface can give an outdoor living space a refined, finished look.

complements your overall style—formal brick or rustic wood chips, for example. A detached patio makes a good retreat, separate from the business of the household. Even though it's situated away from the house, your detached patio should have the same general tone as the house. Its distance from the home lets you create stunning patterns in the surface that won't interfere with the overall design.

COURTYARD: A courtyard is a great solution for townhouses, condos, apartments or homes with small lots. A courtyard needs walls, but if you don't have them, make them—with fencing or tall hedges. Garden beds or planter boxes will make this spot your private oasis, but if garden beds won't do, use potted plants or small trees to bring greenery and flowers into the space. Install trellises and let vines climb the walls. You can even add the splash of falling water by installing a small fountain, available in your garden center. If running water lines and putting in a pump isn't feasible, consider an ornamental wall fountain. Keep the paving subdued and the furniture simple to avoid overwhelming the space.

LEGALITIES

Building codes, zoning ordinances, and deed restrictions can have a major effect on where you put your patio. A little preliminary research will save you time, effort, and much frustration later.

BUILDING CODES: Almost all communities have local building codes to ensure safety and uniformity of building quality. In some communities, patios are considered permanent additions, and you may find regulations that define footing depths, material choices, and fence heights. Check with your local building department before you start, and submit your plans for approval.

ZONING ORDINANCES: Ordinances govern the use of property and the placement of structures on it. They can establish minimum setbacks from property lines, utility easements, and the size of your patio. In recent years, many communities have become strict about the size of patio surface areas— large areas increase runoff into storm sewers.

DEED RESTRICTIONS: Some communities have adopted deed restrictions to maintain control over local property values or architectural style. You may find restraints on the kind of patio you want to build, its style, and the materials you want to use.

UTILITY LINES: Although not technically a legal requirement, the placement of utility lines on your property may affect your patio location. Telephone, gas, electric, and cable television lines may pass through your site, and even if they're deeper than the depth you will excavate for your patio, you don't want to restrict future access by covering them. Check before you start.

DESIGNING FOR YOUR HOME AND YARD

Casual chairs and a scattered paver design balance the more formal look of a raised pool in this patio, making it inviting and comfortable for all occasions.

In scenery characteristic of the desert, the house and pool offer the comforts associated with modern living. The design is formal, but uses organic shapes. Like most successful patio designs, this one is built to fit its surroundings—not contradict them.

The characteristics of your yard and climate will also affect the location and structure of your patio.

YARD INVENTORY

Look out at that vast wilderness of your yard. You'll recognize both limitations and creative possibilities for a patio. If the terrain is flat, building a patio will not be complicated. But if the yard is sloped dramatically, you may have to level it and build retaining walls with a drainage system—or pick another location.

What about mature trees? Build around them. Their height and mass will balance the horizontal expanse of your patio surface. Other existing features, such as flower beds, foundation plantings, fences, walls, and walkways will affect your location. If you can't part with them, and are certain of your favorite patio location, integrate them into your design.

A TOUCH OF FROST

In climates that experience frequent freezing and thawing cycles, you will need to excavate and pour footings for mortared surfaces. Without a concrete base, the surface will heave and crack.

LOCAL EXPERTISE

If you're unsure about where to locate your patio, don't feel you know enough about the environment, or just can't make up your mind about what plants or materials would look best, hire a landscape designer for a brief on-site consultation. Professional advice can work wonders, even if you plan to do the work yourself. Check your phone book listings under "Landscape Architects" or "Landscape Design."

What kind of soil do you have? Loose, loamy soil drains well and is good for plantings. It's easy to excavate but subject to erosion. Silted soil is also easy to dig, but posts will need concrete support. Compact clay soil sheds water, so it can cause runoff problems. You may need to add drainage to patios on clay soil.

DRAINAGE

Standing water isn't welcome on any patio. It spoils your fun and damages your handiwork. And, misguided runoff from a patio adjacent to your house can threaten your home's foundation. Slope the patio gently away from the house—an inch of slope for every four feet of patio. If your landscaping includes terraces or retaining walls, provide drainage to protect your patio. Plantings at the edges of your patio will absorb and slow runoff. As you plan your landscape, don't create narrow channels; they invite erosion.

This hidden sanctuary provides a peaceful setting for quiet conversation, reading, or bird-watching. The irregular pattern of the flagstones adds to the random, natural feeling of the design.

Inspired by the terraced gardens of the Mediterranean, the dry-stacked, stone-wall terraces and slate pavers set in sand create an air of informal dignity. The entire patio feels as if it has been there for many years.

DESIGNING FOR YOUR HOME AND YARD
continued

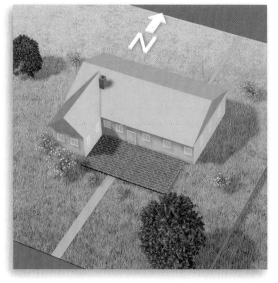

Most homeowners use their patios in the afternoon and evening more than any other time of the day. A south-facing surface, as shown here, can be scorching without an overhead shade structure or trees.

Taking advantage of the way your property is arranged can give you a site with just the amount of sun and shade you want. An east-facing patio, as shown here, will be shaded sooner than any other location.

Even if the north side of your house is not naturally shaded by trees, it will still be in the shadow of the house for the better part of the day. As such, north locations should be planned with care so they have enough light when you want it.

CLIMATE AND WEATHER

To enjoy your patio for as much of the year as possible, pay attention to weather patterns and design your patio so you'll have maximum comfort in a variety of conditions.

SUN AND SHADE: As the sun travels overhead throughout the day and year, the amount of warmth and light you receive will vary. Shadows cast by trees, walls, and rooflines also will shift. Place your patio so these natural patterns correspond to the times of day and seasons when you'll want to use it.

■ For breakfast in the early light, an east-facing patio is ideal: The eastern sun warms the cool morning air. An east-facing site also offers a cool place for evening meals.

■ A west-facing patio will get the hot afternoon sun and without natural—or added—shade, may become unbearably hot.

■ Southern sites get sun all day and also may need added shade. An overhead or vine-covered arbor may be the solution, and the shade will move in a dappled pattern from morning to evening. In the northern hemisphere during winter, the sun's arc is shorter and lower in the sky. Outdoor spaces on the south side of your property will have the best chance of getting any winter sun in mild winter climates.

■ A north-side patio will get sun only if it's located well beyond the shadow line of the house and will probably be cool on all but the hottest days.

A west-facing patio will bear the brunt of the hot afternoon sun. You'll have plenty of sunshine, but you and your guests might roast without trees or an overhead structure. Patio surfaces will radiate heat long after dusk.

WIND: Wind will affect your patio comfort as much as the sun. Soft breezes are delightful, but strong winds are not. Study the wind patterns in your yard and learn to make a distinction between prevailing winds (the general direction of wind currents) and seasonal breezes (those localized to a time of day or season).

If possible, locate your patio in a spot that's sheltered from the most frequent effects of strong winds. You may want to allow breezes to flow across your patio to cool and freshen the air. Slatted fences or windbreaks (trees and hedges) will break up strong winds and let the breeze pass through.

RAIN AND WINTER WEATHER:
You can't block or divert the rain, but you can build yourself some shelter. A solid roof over a part of your patio can keep you dry outdoors in rainy weather. So can a gazebo or retractable awning. If you live in an area with strong winters, remember to construct roof overhangs so they won't be vulnerable to snow buildup or ice dams. Remember to retract the awning before the first snow.

WILDLIFE: Any plantings you add to your design may attract wildlife, even in the cities. Songbirds are colorful, and backyard bird-watching can be a relaxing daily event. Place feeders off the patio area to reduce your cleanup chores. Squirrels, rabbits, raccoons, and deer also may be frequent guests. Fences and certain plants can help protect your patio and garden from damage caused by too frequent visitations. Ask your garden center staff for help with plant selections.

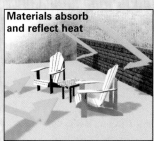

House design will affect your ability to work with the elements. Shade an open structure with an overhead or trees. Where roof overhangs or other covers are already in place, they provide a built-in setting for outdoor living space. Ideally, your patio design should work with what you have.

PATIO MICROCLIMATES

In addition to your area's general weather conditions, your patio also will generate its own microclimates. Your paving materials will both absorb and reflect heat from the sun, and will release heat when the ambient temperature drops, particularly at night.

The height of your patio—or of the different heights in multi-level settings—also will affect its temperature. Cool air, which is heavier than hot air, will flow downhill to create cold pockets and small cooling breezes that flow rapidly across patios tucked against steep hillsides. Use this to your advantage.

Choose lighter-colored paving materials to reflect sunlight and heat, or darker-colored paving materials to absorb and store heat. You also can use organic fill, such as grass or moss, between paved areas to moderate the amount of heat your patio will absorb.

Cool air from hillside

Materials absorb and reflect heat

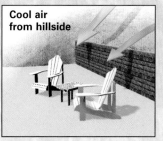

One location can react to varying weather conditions in very different ways. This site gets currents of cool air from the hill, heat and light from the sun reflected off the pavers and the retaining wall, and residual heat radiating from the paved surfaces.

Stored heat radiates

CHOOSING MATERIALS

Materials selection goes hand in hand with planning the form, function, style, and location for your patio. You may be surprised—or even overwhelmed at first—at the range of options available in building materials. If you stay flexible about your design in the early planning stages, you can easily discover materials that have unique qualities—shape, size, color, and texture—that will give your patio the look and feel you'll enjoy most.

Of course, materials vary greatly in the ease of installation, durability, maintenance requirements, and suitability to your climate and drainage. Don't choose something just because you like the way it looks. Ask questions about the other aspects of your choices—maintenance and suitability to your climate, for example. Your materials supplier can suggest alternatives that meet your specific requirements.

Finally, there's always the matter of cost. A patio project will include costs for surface materials, foundation and fillers, and shipping and delivery fees. Choose materials that fit your needs, and create an appealing space that you can build, afford, and enjoy for years.

HOW MUCH WILL YOU NEED?

No matter what kind of surface you choose, you'll need to know the area of your patio (the square footage of its surface) and—for gravel, sand, and concrete—the volume of material to order. Here's a quick review of formulas.

RECTANGULAR PATIOS:
■ *Area:* Length × width (in feet). Example: A 12×16-foot patio=192 square feet.
■ *Volume:* Multiply area by depth. Example: For a 6-inch (half a foot) gravel base in the above patio, 96 cubic feet of gravel (192×0.5=96) is needed.

CIRCULAR PATIOS:
■ *Area:* Multiply the radius (the distance from the center to the edge) by itself and the result by 3.14. Example: A circular patio 24 feet across=452.16 square feet (12×12 × 3.14= 452.16).
■ *Volume:* Area × height. This circular patio needs 226.08 cubic feet of gravel for a 6-inch base.

COMPLEX SHAPES:
■ *Area:* Divide the shape into rectangles and circles, apply the above formulas to each section, and add the results together. Or draw your patio shape on graph paper, with each square representing one square foot. Count the squares, including partial squares in your total.

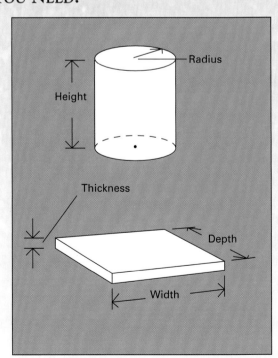

SOURCES FOR MATERIALS

Start your search for materials at their source—brickworks, stone yards, cement plants, landscaping centers, and tile retailers. You'll discover a range of options in color, texture, shape, price, durability, and ease of installation. Seeing the materials will also help you get a better feel for what you like best.

Once you've narrowed your decision to a few choices, get samples (sometimes they're available for free) and bring them back to your patio site. This will help you visualize how the textures and colors will relate to your house and yard.

The Internet is a good source for materials research. Many manufacturers and retailers now have web sites that offer useful reference information about quality, uses, and cost.

An expert can review your plans and site and offer guidance for your selection of materials. An early consultation with a landscape designer can give you confidence as well as new ideas, and may save you hours of effort.

SURFACE MATERIALS

Tiles and pavers combined with red, gold, and earth tones can be especially warm and inviting. They work well with redwood, shredded bark, and other natural materials.

Each material you pick for your patio has unique characteristics and methods of installation. Make sure your choices meet your design needs and that your skills are equal to the installation requirements.

MATERIAL QUALITIES

COLOR: Color does more than establish a link with your home. It helps set the visual mood. Reds, beiges, rusts, browns, yellows, and oranges generally set a warm tone, and complement traditional settings. Blues, grays, or blacks set cooler tones and work well with contemporary designs. Remember that fillers—mortars, sand, and moss or other plants—add color, too. So will furniture. Scale also affects color: Color recedes in small quantities, but can be overpowering in large areas.

TEXTURE: Surface textures also affect patio style and function.

SMOOTH OR ROUGH: Smooth surfaces are great for dancing and also are less absorbent than rough materials, so they resist stains. However, smooth materials, such as glazed tile, polished stone, smoothly troweled concrete—even wood—are slick when wet. Polished surfaces can assault you with glare in direct sunlight. The surface variation in natural stone will give your patio a natural or old-fashioned look. Poured concrete offers the flattest, least varied surface, but even concrete can be textured.

HARD OR SOFT: Brick, tile, and concrete surfaces are hard, but alternatives such as loose gravel, rock beds, wood chips, and bark offer softer, more comfortable options that give way when you walk on them. They make rustic complements to woodland or informal settings.

CARE AND HANDLING

INSTALLATION: Loose materials are the easiest to install; just excavate, level a sand base, and pour in the surface material. Brick, flagstone, and concrete pavers (not tile) dry-set in sand or in a sand-and-mortar base require more excavation, a deeper sand base, and patient layout. This method takes time and requires more patience than skill. So do flagstone and wood rounds inlaid individually in the soil. Patios with materials (brick, flagstone, concrete pavers, and tile) set with a mortar base demand extensive excavation (you're actually making two patios, one under the other), moderate to high skills, and a work crew. The same is true of poured concrete patios.

MAINTENANCE: Factor in longevity and maintenance to your material decisions. Properly set in a level and cured mortar base, brick and stone will last a lifetime. Wood finishes and loose material require yearly maintenance and frequent replacement and are subject to moss growth (it's slippery) in humid climates. Sandstone and limestone can crack in hard winters and will need replacement.

WET OR DRY BASES?

Dry paving techniques, in which modular units like brick, stone, or pavers are placed into leveled sand bases, are generally easier than installations that require concrete or mortar. Dry-set surfaces require periodic maintenance. Mortared surfaces require more skill and a bigger budget. But they are virtually maintenance free (although sandstone and limestone may crack), and if properly laid, most will last a lifetime.

Choose patio materials the way you choose an outfit. Either make the parts match exactly or make them so different that the combination appears to be purposeful.

Materials set in sand are relatively maintenance-free in the first few years, but require sand replacement over time. Joints filled with plants or grass will need weeding or mowing.

DECISIONS, DECISIONS...

DO IT YOURSELF? You can answer this question based on costs alone, but give some thought to other factors.

■ Be thorough when analyzing costs. The total cost of your patio will include not only the price of your surface materials but also shipping and delivery charges. Include the costs of edging, foundation and filler material, landscaping elements, and the costs of purchasing or renting tools. Remember the cost of decorative elements, including lighting and furniture. Even if you plan to build your patio yourself, you may need to pay for professional assistance for certain portions of it, such as design consultation.

Now compare your total do-it-yourself costs to the costs for contracting the job. Expect to pay 100 percent more for contracted work—less in areas where labor costs are low.

■ Make sure you have the skills needed to install the materials. Think about how much experience and knowledge you have now, how much you're willing to learn, and how much time you can devote to construction. Will you complete your project in a single period, or do you prefer to take your time?

■ Now look on the positive side. There are some things money can't buy. Doing it yourself will be an investment in your quality of life, and nothing beats the pride of accomplishment. Your increased skill level will prepare you for other projects, and the satisfaction of learning a new skill will stay with you for a long time.

SAVINGS: Once you decide to do all (or part of) the work yourself, try to cut costs.

■ Buy the best materials you can afford. High-quality materials last longer and provide the highest return on your investment. Bring the materials to the site yourself. If the supplier is delivering, make sure your order is palleted or in protected bundles to prevent breakage and to avoid replacement costs.

■ Keep an open mind as you learn about materials. Research can lead you to more affordable options.

■ Shop around. Visit several suppliers; get samples and quotes.

You can often save money by buying your paving materials directly from quarries or manufacturers, especially if they're located in your area.

HIDING WEAR?

Consider cleaning requirements when you choose materials. Very light or very dark surfaces will show stains and scuffs more than muted, mottled surface colors.

BRICK

The bricks in this expansive patio complement the clapboard siding, cedar shakes, and rough stone wall. Traditional materials often are used to blend with an older home, but brick works well in contemporary designs, too.

	Low	Moderate	High
Affordability			
Simplicity			
Durability			
Versatility			

Brick's warm and earthy colors lend an old-world flavor to patios. Manufacturers offer hundreds of styles, sizes, densities, and colors. Expect to pay a premium for custom-ordered or unusually colored brick. Other brick is moderately priced—between wood and stone.

Brick is one of the most goof-proof patio paving materials for the homeowner to install—especially set in sand. Its dimensions are proportional to each other and consistent among each style. This simplifies the process of measuring, estimating quantities, and installation. A well-built brick patio, set in sand or mortar, requires minimal upkeep—or none at all.

TYPES OF BRICK

Some brick is made for building walls and some for facing structures. You'll want either severe weather (SW) or moderate weather (MW) grades, depending on your climate.
PAVING BRICK: Paving brick is made of very dense clay fired to high temperatures.

It is hard, durable, and less likely to absorb water and crack from freezing.
COMMON BRICK: Sometimes called building brick, common brick is designed for general-purpose building. Though it's more porous than paving brick, you can use it as patio paving in milder climates and for surfaces that will not get heavy use.
USED BRICK: Brick salvaged from old buildings or street pavements is an attractive and moderately inexpensive alternative for use in moderate climates. Buy extra for replacements in sand-based patios.

Check your building supply center for brick pavers that are molded and stained to look like salvaged brick.

BRICK PATTERNS

Brick lends itself easily to a wide range of patterns. Two of the easiest patterns to create are called "running bond" and "jack on jack," with more complex patterns sometimes requiring bricks of varying sizes or cut shapes.

Sketch patterns on graph paper or cut cardboard shapes for trial layouts. Better yet, get samples of several bricks to explore patterns before you commit to a final design.

Make the design more interesting: Set different patterns in alternating sections, alternate brick colors, or edge your patio with concrete, redwood timbers, or railroad ties.

EXAMPLES: The most common brick patterns are shown at right, but they are not your only choices. These patterns use standard sizes and proportions, which makes them easier for beginners.

INSTALLATION

Brick can be set in sand, mortar, or a combination of sand and dry mortar. Brick patios set in sand need a 4-inch gravel and a 2-inch sand base. Mortared brick patios require 4 inches of gravel under a 4-inch concrete pad. For setting all types of paving bricks, you will need to excavate the patio site to the depth equal to the thickness of the material plus the sand or gravel base (and the mortar for hard-set surfaces).

SAND: Setting brick in a sand base requires only simple skills, plenty of patience to create, and some care to maintain.

DRY MORTAR: In this variation, a mix of sand and dry cement is swept into the joints between the bricks. After the mix is dampened, it sets as a solid mortar filling.

WET MORTAR: You'll need to mix mortar and lay bricks quickly and carefully into a bed of wet mortar. The process calls for skill, patience, accuracy, and speed.

CALCULATING QUANTITIES

1. Figure out the area, in square feet, that you need to pave (*see note about measuring surface area, page 16*).
2. Ask your supplier for the actual dimensions of the bricks you choose, as well as the recommended number of bricks per square foot.
3. Multiply the area of your patio by the number of bricks needed for each square foot.
4. Add five percent to your total so that you will have enough extra bricks to allow for errors.
5. If the supplier has a generous return policy, round your order up to the nearest pallet size.

RUNNING BOND

JACK ON JACK

BASKET WEAVE

HERRINGBONE

PINWHEEL

SPIRAL

HOW TO ORDER

WHERE: Brickyards; building centers; masonry, landscape, and patio suppliers.

YELLOW PAGES: Under "Brick," "Masonry," "Building Materials."

QUANTITIES: Sold singly or in pallets of 100 or 500.

DELIVERY FORMAT: Order on pallets to protect bricks from breaking when they're unloaded.

SAND FOR DRY SET: 20 pounds of washed concrete sand provides a 2-inch layer for 1 square foot of paving.

SUBBASE: 50 pounds of class-5 gravel provides a 4-inch-deep gravel foundation for 1 square foot of paving.

CONCRETE FOR THE BASE: Ask your supplier for advice on concrete quantities and mortar for the mortar bed.

FLAGSTONE

By using fewer and larger flagstones, the owner of this patio created a bit of drama in an unassuming corner of the yard. The size, color, and layout of the stone make the small patio inviting and attractive.

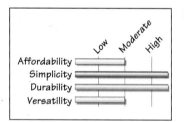

	Low	Moderate	High
Affordability			
Simplicity			
Durability			
Versatility			

HEAVY BUT FRAGILE

Because flagstone is heavy, make sure that the pallets are placed close to the patio site. Also, make sure you keep a sturdy wheelbarrow on hand for moving individual stones.

The term "flagstone" covers a variety of flat, natural stone that is sawed into slabs, and then either cut or broken into shapes for use as paving. Flagstone includes many types of stone but the most common are granite, bluestone, redstone, sandstone, limestone, and slate.

Flagstone can have bright or subdued colors and comes in irregular or cut rectangular shapes. It lends itself to free-form layouts and geometric patterns. It appeals to many homeowners because it is durable and easy to maintain. Its surface is rougher than brick or concrete, however, and it is more expensive—from 5 to 10 times more.

Don't hurry when you choose flagstone. Find the flagstone you like best and the color, texture, and pattern that complements your design. Flagstone fits many design styles, and is frequently installed where a rustic, hand-hewn look is desired.

TYPES TO CONSIDER

Each kind of flagstone has distinct physical qualities, all varieties are cut in ½- to 2-inch thicknesses.

GRANITE: generally smooth, sometimes pitted, very hard, slippery when wet (especially if polished)—red, brown, grey, black.

SANDSTONE: porous, high amounts of compressed sand, absorbs water, and can crack in freezing winters—red, brown, tan.
LIMESTONE: chalky and porous, seems soft to the touch, absorbs water, and cracks in freezing weather—brown, tan.
SLATE: fine grained, smooth to rough, very dense, slippery when wet—grey, black, blue.

BUYING STONE

Different suppliers have different names for the same kinds of stone. To avoid confusion, don't shop over the phone. Go to the suppliers and look at actual samples. Ask questions about where the stone is quarried. That will help you estimate relative shipping costs and select native stone if your design is regional.

Most suppliers will be glad to talk about their products. Find quarries or suppliers and buy the stone you want directly from them to save money.

PATTERNS AND INSTALLATION

■ Set flagstone free-form in a wide variety of configurations in sand, dry mortar, or on a concrete base. You also can dig separate holes and set each flagstone in the soil. Dry-set flagstone does not require advanced masonry skills; but mortared installations on a concrete base may call for some experienced help and a labor crew, especially if the patio is large and the base is poured ready-mix.
■ Flagstone patterns require careful planning. As you'll see in a later chapter *(see page 58)*, a trial layout on the grass is time well spent. Designs that leave small, irregular spaces are very attractive; but you will want your results to look natural, so fit the stones carefully. Use large stones to set your basic pattern and fill in the spaces between them with stones of smaller sizes. If you can't find a piece with a specific shape and size, cut it to create the shape you need.

HOW TO ORDER

WHERE: Local quarries or stone, building, landscape, or patio suppliers.
YELLOW PAGES: Look under "Stone," "Landscape Contractors and Suppliers," "Building Materials," "Patios."
QUANTITIES: Order by the square foot or ton; 1 ton of stone (eighty 25-pound pieces) should be enough for up to 120 square feet of surface area.
DELIVERY FORMAT: Order flagstone on pallets to protect it from breaking when unloaded. Check the stones after they're delivered. Because natural stone varies widely, batches can contain cracked, oddly shaped, or too many small stones. Send rejects back to the supplier in exchange for better quality stones. You also can ask to handpick stones from supply yards.
SAND FOR DRY SET: 20 pounds of well-graded, washed concrete sand will provide a 2-inch layer for every square foot of paved surface.
SUBBASE: 50 pounds of class-5 gravel will provide a

4-inch-deep foundation for 1 square foot of paved surface. Ask your supplier to help you figure concrete amounts for a mortared surface foundation.

CONCRETE PAVERS

Using only three shapes designed to fit together, the concrete pavers in this patio form an elegant circle. The builder gently raised the center of the circle to create a patio surface that quickly drains in all directions.

	Low	Moderate	High
Affordability			
Simplicity			
Durability			
Versatility			

As patio building materials, concrete pavers offer several advantages. They are widely available, less expensive than other materials, lightweight, and durable under even heavy use. They used to be made only in gray 1-foot squares. Not any more. Concrete pavers are sold in a wide variety of shapes, sizes, earth-tone colors (grays and off whites, too), and finishes. Concrete pavers will harmonize with almost any architectural style, and can be a few inches to several feet across.

SHAPES AND SURFACES: Made from very dense, pressure-formed, cast concrete, concrete pavers come in circles, rectangles, diamonds, hexagons, octagons, crescents— and more. You'll find smooth, textured, stamp-patterned, and aggregate surfaces. You can even buy pavers that look remarkably like brick, stone, adobe, marble, or cobblestone.

DURABILITY: Typically thinner than brick (1½ to 2½ inches thick), concrete pavers can support heavy loads and withstand the effects of extreme climates.

VERSATILITY: Whether you're creating an entire patio surface, a simple border, or a partially paved area mixed with garden, moss, or loose filler, there's a concrete paver to suit your needs. Weave different styles and colors together, or combine them with brick, wood, poured concrete, or natural stone.

TYPES

Concrete pavers are difficult to categorize by shape or color, but fit into categories defined by the method of installation.

SKIN DEEP

Look closely at the pigment of pavers. A shallow color can wear off quickly, exposing bare concrete. Buy pavers that have pigment impregnated throughout their thickness.

INTERLOCKING PAVERS: Interlocking pavers resist lateral movement because the sides—contoured, more than four-sided, S-shape, or crescents—work against each other to keep the pavers stable. They'll remain firmly in place even under heavy use and severe changes in weather. Each shape combines with others to form simple or elaborate patterns. Corner- and end-piece pavers are great for finishing edges.

REGULAR PAVERS: Regular or standard pavers are rectangular and not as stable as interlocking pavers. You may find them shifting over time, especially if your patio gets hard use. You can arrange them in interesting patterns, but their variety is more limited than what you can achieve with interlocking pavers.

TURF BLOCKS: These pavers have holes in which to plant grass or ground cover, and they make especially attractive walkways. They will even support the weight of a car in distinctive grass driveways.

INSTALLATION

It's the paver shape that creates the pattern, and you need to pay close attention to its scale. A small-paver pattern can get too busy if spread over a large patio, but a small patio set with overly large pavers will appear dwarfed.

Concrete pavers set in sand need a 4-inch gravel and a 2-inch sand base. Mortared pavers require 4 inches of gravel under a 4-inch concrete pad.

MAKE YOUR OWN

Customize your own concrete pavers in 2×4 forms. You will be limited to rectangular shapes, but adding aggregate, texturing, or color lets you create unique options. Homemade pavers won't be as durable, but may be just right if you can't find ready-made materials.

HOW TO ORDER

WHERE: Building supply centers; concrete suppliers; landscape suppliers; or lawn, garden, and patio stores.

YELLOW PAGES: Look under "Concrete Products," "Building Materials," "Landscape Supplies," or "Patios."

QUANTITIES: Order pavers individually, by the square foot, or in larger, pre-grouped quantities called cubes or bands (enough for 16 lineal feet).

DELIVERY FORMAT: Order in banded cubes to protect pavers from breaking when they're unloaded.

SAND FOR DRY SET: 20 pounds of well-graded and washed sand will provide a 2-inch layer of sand for each square foot of paved surface.

SUBBASE: 50 pounds of class-5 gravel will provide a 4-inch-deep gravel foundation for each square foot of paved surface. Ask your supplier for help in figuring concrete for mortared patios.

NOTE: Make sure the pavers you order are intended specifically for the use you have in mind.

POURED CONCRETE

Concrete doesn't have to look institutional. Four poured slabs divided by single lines of brick make this landing a place to pause on the way into or out of the house. A carefully applied texture helps the concrete blend in with the stone wall and wooden deck.

	Low	Moderate	High
Affordability			
Simplicity			
Durability			
Versatility			

Poured concrete is one of the most versatile patio materials available. It will conform to almost any shape when wet and will support the weight of tall buildings when cured. You can finish it with dozens of colors and textures, or stamp it to resemble other materials, such as brick or natural stone.

Poured concrete offers an affordable way to create large patio areas, but it is very tricky to handle. While novices may find it more difficult to work with than modular materials such as brick, stone, tile, or concrete pavers, concrete appeals to skilled builders because they must mix, pour, and finish a large area in a single day.

FINISHES

Decorative surfaces not only will help you avoid concrete's institutional gray, but they also will improve traction.

WHAT'S IN CONCRETE

1 part portland cement (a fine mixture of clay and limestone)
$2\frac{1}{4}$ to $2\frac{1}{2}$ parts clean construction sand
$2\frac{1}{2}$ to 3 parts coarse aggregate (gravel or rock)
$\frac{1}{2}$ part clean water

AGGREGATE: A pebbly texture created by the addition of smooth stones in the surface.
TROWELED: Swirls made with a finishing trowel add interest and increase traction.
BROOMED: A damp, stiff garage broom pulled across the wet surface makes this patterned slip-resistant surface.
TRAVERTINE: Resembles finished marble, absorbs water and cracks in hard winters.
ROCK SALT: A pitted surface created by rolling rock salt before the concrete cures. Not for hard winters.
SEMI-SMOOTH: A surface slightly roughened with a wood float. Good skid resistance.
SMOOTH: Slippery when wet, but good for dance parties. Finished with a metal trowel.
STAMPED: Geometric patterns created by metal stamps (you can rent them) to resemble natural stone, tile, or brick.

LIMITATIONS

Poured concrete isn't perfect. Here's why:
■ It must be mixed to specifications or the mix will weaken or disintegrate.
■ Very smooth finishes can make a patio dangerously slippery when wet.
■ Concrete surfaces are not as resistant to cracking as stone, brick, tile, or pavers.
■ Large areas reflect heat and can make the patio uncomfortable.
■ Installation requires some skill and a well-coordinated work crew. Concrete sets in about two hours, depending on the weather.
■ Errors in concrete are almost impossible to correct; they can't be pulled out and set down again like brick, tile, or pavers.

Think carefully about your skills, time, and design needs before you choose to use concrete.

ADDED INGREDIENTS

If your climate treats you to wide variations in temperature and strong or frequent freeze and thaw cycles, you'll need to add additional ingredients to your mix that will allow the concrete to expand and contract without cracking. Ask your vendor to recommend additives for use in your climate.

MIXING OPTIONS

BULK DRY INGREDIENTS: Take a look at "What's in Concrete" on the opposite page. You can buy these ingredients separately and mix them together with water—by hand in a mortar box or wheelbarrow, or in a rented concrete mixer. Mixing concrete is a heavy job that requires a strong hoe and stamina, but for small jobs it's economical.
PREMIX: An easier but somewhat more costly alternative is to buy concrete in bags with the dry ingredients mixed in the correct proportions. You just add water, mix, and pour. Premix takes the guesswork out of mixing— but not the effort. It makes jobs under a cubic yard manageable (you'll need 40 to 50 bags, depending on the weight), but for anything larger than that, order ready-mix.
READY-MIX: Ready-mix relieves you of the mixing process, but requires coordination of a hardy and experienced work crew. Your site must be accessible to a large truck, and ready for the pour as soon as it arrives. Ready-mix will come with additives that will make it workable in a variety of weather conditions.

HOW TO ORDER

WHERE: Building supply centers, concrete suppliers, landscape suppliers, patio supply stores.
YELLOW PAGES: Look under "Concrete Products," "Building Materials," "Landscape Equipment," or "Patios."
DELIVERY QUANTITIES: Concrete is sold by the cubic yard. Your vendor will need the area and depth of your patio and will bring the correct amount. A cubic yard will pour a 4-inch slab on an 85-square-foot patio.
TYPICAL DELIVERY CHARGES: Included.
DELIVERY FORMAT: Delivered by large trucks; access to the patio avoids hauling in wheelbarrows.
SUBBASE: 50 pounds of class-5 gravel will provide a 4-inch-deep foundation for each square foot of paved surface.

TILE

For a house with a clay tile roof and a colored stucco exterior, ceramic tile is the obvious choice for the patio. Beds and pots of flowers add contrast in shape and color.

	Low	Moderate	High
Affordability			
Simplicity			
Durability			
Versatility			

The beauty and tactile appeal of ceramic tile is unique among materials. Made from thin panels of high-fired clay, ceramic tiles are extremely durable and offer more variety in colors, shapes, and sizes than do other materials. Here are some other advantages:

■ They absorb very little water and are resistant to cracking in changing temperatures. Once restricted to warm climates, there are now newer varieties that are practical in many more climates.

■ Unglazed tile is less likely to be slick when it's wet, which means the patio surface will be safer after it rains. Glazed tiles are for decorative uses only and are dangerously slippery when wet. For best results, use unglazed, textured tile that is made specifically for outdoor paving.

■ The high durability will support heavy loads (but only when properly bedded).

Tile does, however, bring with it some drawbacks. It is more expensive than other

GLAZED TILE

Glazed tile gets too slick when it's wet, so don't use it for paving your patio. However, its glossy look and strong colors can make fine accents for edges and trim, raised beds, or wall decorations.

materials (though with diligent hunting, you can find sale prices of lower quality tile as low as $1.50 per square foot—but beware of bargains). Because it's square, it is more difficult to lay in patterns that are similar to brick.

TYPES OF CERAMIC TILE

Four types of tile are made for outdoor patios:
PATIO OR TERRA-COTTA: Fired ceramic tile with earthen colors and irregular surfaces create pleasant, unobtrusive moods.
QUARRY TILES: Machine-made and formed from dense clay pressed tightly into molds, quarry tile is hard and is available with rounded or sharp edges and corners. Its appearance varies from one brand and firing to another and even within the same firing. Ask your dealer to show you how to judge quality. Then make sure all the tiles you buy have the same lot number—your best ensurance for getting consistent tiles.
TILE PAVERS: These molded tiles are larger than other tiles and are made to cover larger areas. Some are designed to retain the deliberately imperfect look of a hand-crafted item. Mexican pavers, for example, are grainy and unglazed, with rough edges. The earthy colors work well outdoors. Others are regular and modern. Tile pavers are usually more expensive than quarry tiles.
SYNTHETIC STONE TILES: As the name suggests, this type of tile is made of stained

clay bodies that look very much like stone surfaces, such as granite or sandstone. Synthetic tiles are thinner, flatter, lighter, smoother, and more regularly shaped than natural stone and measure either 6 or 12 inches across. They offer a clever alternative for homeowners who want the practical qualities of a synthetic material, yet prefer the look of stone.

INSTALLATION

No matter what type of tile you plan to use, you will need to set it in mortar on a 4-inch concrete slab over a 4-inch gravel base. Because it is thin, tile is susceptible to cracking on uneven surfaces. Make sure the base is absolutely smooth and level. Cracked tiles will only come out with chiseling.

SEALING TILES

Ask your dealer if your tiles have been pre-treated with a sealer at the factory. If not, you'll need to apply a good sealant after they've been set. Repeat this process periodically to protect the tiles from scratches and to keep them from absorbing water. Quality sealants are easy to apply, won't discolor tile, and provide an even, effective seal.

BUYING TILE

WHERE: Tile retailers, ceramic suppliers, home centers; national retailing franchises specialize in tile.
YELLOW PAGES: Look under "Tile," "Ceramic Supplies," or "Patios."
DELIVERY QUANTITIES: Individually, by the square foot, or in boxed cartons of larger quantities.
DELIVERY CHARGES: Moderate to high, depending on location.
DELIVERY FORMAT: Best to order in boxed cartons.
FOUNDATION MATERIALS: 4 inches of gravel subbase (50 pounds of class-5 gravel per 4 inches of depth every square foot) and a 4-inch concrete slab—ready-mix for large patios.
SPECIAL CONSIDERATIONS: Make sure you order extra decorative tile for edges, walls, or trim to limit return trips to the vendor.

WOOD

Wood brings a warmth to patios in a way that no other material can match. It imparts an appealing, organic feel to a patio and can be set in sand or soil—or pieced into boxed units in slightly raised walkways or platforms.

Treated landscape timbers, wide wooden rounds, and end-grain blocks that look like bricks are found in patio designs that have a woodland atmosphere. You can install wood decking squares (they look like parquet) in square or rectangular beds, or use wood rounds in free-form layouts set within larger areas of grass, plants, or moss.

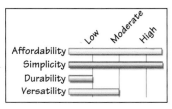

	Low	Moderate	High
Affordability			
Simplicity			
Durability			
Versatility			

With a few weekends of work and a modest supply of redwood, homeowners transformed this shady spot into a wooded hideaway.

HOW TO ORDER

WHERE: Lumberyards, building suppliers, landscape suppliers, garden retailers.
YELLOW PAGES: Look under "Lumber," "Building Materials," or "Landscape Equipment and Supplies."
DELIVERY QUANTITIES: Depends on the type of wood being ordered (total square feet, beam lengths, or individual sections).
DELIVERY CHARGES: Moderate.
DELIVERY FORMAT: By the piece or in bundles.
ORDERING SAND: 20 pounds of well-graded, washed concrete sand will provide a 2-inch layer for each square foot of paved surface.
SPECIAL CONSIDERATIONS: If you plan to use wood as a patio surface, make sure to order edging materials as well.

PROTECTIVE MEASURES

Wood is readily available and affordable, but is susceptible to damage from insects, mildew, and rot. Over time, wood also may splinter and crack. To prevent common kinds of damage to wood in outdoor structures, take these steps:

■ Select rot-resistant and insect-resistant varieties, such as redwood, cedar, or cypress.
■ Buy pressure-treated lumber (.40 grade) rated for direct ground contact.
■ Set wood in sand and gravel beds to allow for good drainage.
■ Clean a wood patio regularly; use fungicide to remove mold, mildew, and fungus.
■ Treat lumber with appropriate varnishes or sealants—before you install it.

INSTALLATION

Imbed single wood rounds and blocks directly in the soil, or better yet, in a 2-inch sand base for drainage. Mount squares and boards on low frames directly on grade.

Treated lumber has a greenish cast that weathers gray—you also can stain it. It contains an arsenic compound, so wear long sleeves, gloves, and a respirator to minimize exposure to the sawdust when cutting and handling it.

LOOSE MATERIALS

Loose materials offer an alternative to hard pavements. Used either as a primary paving material or in combination with harder surfaces, loose materials offer an environmentally friendly means (many products are recycled materials) of creating paths, open settings, and transitional surfaces between harder pavements and garden areas. Loose materials are generally available at low cost, and most require little maintenance.

■ Unlike harder paving surfaces, loose paving materials will shift beneath your feet to enhance your walking comfort and to give your patio the feeling of a pleasant park or a spot in the woods.

■ The most popular loose materials for patio surfaces are easy to install and maintain, and offer many appealing design possibilities.

■ One additional benefit of loose materials is that they provide better drainage than any they other surfaces. This helps prevent erosion and, except for wood products, makes the patio area easier to use after a rainfall.

Here are some of the more popular loose paving materials.

PEA GRAVEL: This material consists of medium-sized stones that have been naturally smoothed by river or lake water. River rock is available in many colors, and it shifts easily under foot. It also has a visually soft look that can be raked in interesting furrows and lines.

CRUSHED STONE: This is quarried rock that has been mechanically crushed and then graded so that most of the stones are of a similar size, with varying shapes and colors.

WOOD BARK, CHIPS, NUGGETS, AND SHREDS: Several types of wood—including redwood, cedar, cypress, and pine—are available in chipped and shredded forms. Redwood, cedar, and cypress are naturally resistant to the effects of weather and insects. Wood chips can serve a variety of landscaping

Challenge your imagination when combining loose and hard paving materials in your patio and garden. Consider concrete pavers set in beds of river rock or pea gravel, wood rounds in beds of chips, widely spaced sections of brick, tile, or pavers interspersed with channels of pea gravel or rock, or broad gravel patios or contained pathways lined with flagstones.

purposes, particularly as mulch around plants, shrubs, and trees. They also care useful for cushioning surfaces under children's play equipment.

However, wood chips and other loose materials that are relatively light can be pushed out of place by footsteps. Add edging such as railroad ties, brick, pavers, or stone.

	Low	Moderate	High
Affordability			
Simplicity			
Durability			
Versatility			

HOW TO ORDER

Wood products are available by the bag at lumberyards, building supply centers, landscape suppliers, and patio supply stores. Or you may be able to get them from your local parks department—for free. Crushed stone and pea gravel can be bought by the ton from quarries, stone suppliers, or patio supply stores. See the Yellow Pages for "Lumber," "Building Materials," "Landscaping," "Quarries," or "Stone."

FOUNDATIONS, FILLERS, AND EDGING

As a bed for brick or concrete pavers, sand is economical and easy to find. To create a level surface that won't sink under the weight of the pavers, pack the sand with a power tamper.

Mortar holds pavers and flagstones in place more securely than sand does, but mortar requires a concrete slab underneath. For tile patios, a mortar bed is the only choice.

River rocks look good next to most patio surfaces. Larger stones make uncomfortable walking surfaces, though, so use them only where you don't expect any foot traffic.

Though hidden from view, foundation materials provide drainage and support to keep paved surfaces from cracking under weight or stress. Foundations are essential for the long-term stability of your patio and will allow surface materials to shift in a unit as the ground freezes and thaws. This keeps the surface material from cracking.

Fillers between the joints secure the blocks, bricks, tiles, or stone, but they are more than functional. Their color and texture should be an integral part of your design.

FOUNDATION MATERIALS

CLASS-5 GRAVEL: Install a 4-inch subbase of compacted gravel for all foundations—mortared or dry-set. The gravel should be small, fine, and granular, so it packs down tightly without air pockets.
SAND: Over the gravel base, dry-set patios need a 2-inch bed of sand for the pavers. Level the sand with a 2×4.
POURED CONCRETE: Concrete is not used for dry-set patios, but is the stabilizing element for all mortared surfaces. You'll need a 4-inch slab poured over the gravel subbase (you won't use sand in the foundation for mortared patios).
WELDED-WIRE REINFORCING MESH: You'll need this to reinforce any concrete pad you're pouring for a mortared surface.
LANDSCAPE FABRIC: Put this over the gravel base to keep weeds from growing up through dry-set surfaces. You won't need it for mortared work.

FILLERS

SAND: For a surface of pavers or stones set on a sand bed, additional washed sand makes an ideal filler material. Add new sand at least once a year to keep the joints filled.
MORTAR: This is what adheres the brick, stone, or tile to the concrete pad—and the paving pieces to each other. You'll need a ¾-inch layer for brick and an inch for stone.
DRY MORTAR: Added dry with sand between joints, then moistened for dry mortared brick and stone.
CRUSHED ROCK: Different kinds and colors of finely crushed rock make an excellent filler between bulkier pavings such as flagstone or wood rounds.

Tamp crushed stone with a 2×4 or any lumber that fits between the paving material.

KEEP YOUR FOOTING

Be careful with moss, plant, and grass fillers. They are very slippery when wet. Also remember that any living fillers will have to be weeded, clipped, or mowed.

EDGING AND DECORATIVE ELEMENTS

Although not required for concrete slabs, flagstone, and mortared surfaces, edgings are a must for dry-set brick and concrete pavers. Something has to hold these loose materials in place, and that's where edging comes in. Edgings also serve an important function—similar to a picture frame, they set off and separate the patio from its surroundings.

Edgings also smooth visual transitions between hard paving and softer lawn and garden areas. Use edging materials that match or that tastefully contrast with the paving materials. Brick is a complement to brick but brings a striking contrast to a loose-filled or poured concrete surface.

FINISHED EDGES

You don't have to limit yourself to edgings installed at grade. For a defining touch, use boulders, benches, bushes, potted plants, flower or herb beds, trees, or paths. Bring color, texture, and even the perfume of flowers to the perimeter of your patio.

Concrete pavers also are designed for edging. Set them straight or in long decorative curves.

Bricks set vertically in trenches or in mortar edging beds break the horizontal pattern of your pavers. Or set them flat, side-by-side.

Wood can be used below grade or at ground level. Use benderboard to curve around corners. Landscaping timbers create straight runs.

Plastic edging strips are flexible and affordable. Cut a narrow trench with a flat-bladed shovel, push the edging in place, and backfill the trench.

If your patio will be surrounded by a garden, you may not want the distinct edge that hard surfaced materials provide. Let your plantings overhang the patio. Shrubs and flowering plants can create a border just as well as landscape timbers or concrete can.

REFINING THE
DETAILS

You've pondered your patio's function and style, and you've chosen the materials you'll use to build it. Before you dive into construction, however, it's important to refine your plan, to clarify and map out precisely where all the final elements will go. Taking the time now to create a carefully detailed plan will save you time, money, and frustration throughout the construction process, and it will increase your satisfaction with your finished patio. If you suspect you could use a little help along the way, enlist the aid of design professionals to review your plans and offer suggestions. They can help you make it better.

WHERE TO LOOK FOR HELP

Even if you're planning to handle the bulk of the construction yourself, consider hiring professionals if:

■ You'd like their input with ideas.
■ You'd like a professionally drawn plan.
■ The terrain is steep or rough.
■ Your patio is complex.
■ You just need a little expert advice or assistance.

There are specialties within the landscaping profession. Here's a brief summary of what each has to offer.

Landscape architects have the most formal training, with college degrees and licenses in landscape architecture. They can handle all aspects of planning and structural work, including detailed plans, solid technical expertise, and construction supervision.

Landscape designers tend to have strong backgrounds in horticulture, and are skilled in other aspects of structural design as well. They can help plan your landscape style and draw plans, but they will not supervise construction.

Landscape contractors are the pros who actually do the clearing, planting, and building required for landscape and patio installations. They may help draw your plans, but their expertise is in construction.

Nursery staff and gardeners can give you suggestions on general landscaping ideas as well as specific information about soils, trees, and plants.

When hiring professionals, make sure you get a written contract—one that will release you and your property from liens and protect you from potential damage or liability for personal injury. Contractors should be insured and bonded; bonding assures you that the work will be completed if the contractor fails to finish the job. If you're doing some of the work yourself, make sure the contract specifies what your responsibilities are and lists completion dates for the tasks both you and the contractor will complete.

Good material selection and a well-drawn plan make the elements of this patio design work in harmony. The flagstone, wood, and plantings contribute to the woodland serenity of this setting.

PLANNING YOUR LANDSCAPE

Take your design experiments off the drawing board and into the yard. Use garden hose, powdered chalk, or acrylic spray paint to outline different patio sizes and locations. Use lightweight lawn furniture as stand-ins for future structures, and helium-filled balloons as imaginary trees and shrubs. Then you can test your ideas with walk-throughs.

Approach obstacles with creativity. Treat the natural features of your yard as opportunities. Work around your trees to make them centerpieces that deliver welcome shade.

The success of your patio site depends on detailed plans. Before you put your ideas on paper, first conduct a tour of your yard. Then you will make a base map, experiment with a bubble design, and finally, develop a plan that shows all the elements in place.

EXPLORING AND MEASURING YOUR PROPERTY

Begin by walking around the outside of your house with a clipboard and a 100-foot steel measuring tape. You'll be measuring and sketching in the outlines of structures and plantings and other major details. Later you will transfer these sketches more exactly to a graph paper map. Even though you're familiar with the basic look of your own house and lot, don't take anything for granted.

START WITH BOUNDARIES: Starting with the exact location of your property lines, (look for metal markers or use a metal detector to find them), sketch in the outline of your house, noting its distance from the property lines. Take accurate measurements from both property lines. Measure and record the dimensions of each wall of your house and the sizes of other structures such as detached garages or sheds. Your sketch should include the distances structures are from one another.

LOOK AT SMALLER ELEMENTS: Include the little things. They will matter when you build your patio. Here's a sample list of items to watch for:

■ Location of doors and windows, including width, height, distance from the ground, and what rooms they lead from.

■ Extension of roof eaves beyond the exterior walls of the house.

■ Location of downspouts and direction of runoff.

■ Where existing trees, shrubs, and gardens are planted.

■ Location of outdoor walls, fences, steps, walks, and driveways.

■ The location of hose bibs, underground sewage systems, catch basins, and septic tanks.

Measure and record the pitch and direction of slopes, steps, and major differences in ground level. Include both the height (the rise) and the length (the run).

TAKE IN THE BROADER VIEW: Now step back and consider the assets and liabilities of your property. Note them along with solutions to problem areas. Make notes of the following items:

■ The distance from your proposed patio to streets, alleys, and sidewalks.

■ The location of street lights and light from neighboring properties.

- Views you want to maintain or block.
- Nearby sources of noise—day and night.
- Additions you need to make to improve your privacy (walls, fences, and shrub or tree plantings).
- Drainage problems you need to correct.
- Locations of new planting beds.

Note any of your neighbors' trees or bushes that overhang or shade your yard and at what times this shading occurs. Even if you can't change them, they will affect the way your patio looks and feels.

LOOK FOR UTILITY LINES

Your patio and attendant landscaping will require excavation, so you need to make sure that you know the exact location of utility lines. Check with each utility—they will give you locations that are precise, marking on the ground the location and run of their lines. Even if your design or local building codes don't require approval by the utility companies, your safety does. Don't take chances when a mistake could be expensive— or dangerous.

Even if safety isn't an issue, you don't want your patio to cover lines and prevent future access. Rights of access by utility companies are called easements, and easements apply whether or not you receive the service of the utility. So, even if you use a satellite dish for television, you need to find out if the cable company uses underground lines: Note all easements on your sketch.

Overhead telephone, cable television, and power lines are not likely to get in the way of your construction project, but if your design includes tall structures or new trees, make sure they won't hit the overhead lines.

Let your patio reflect your region. Here, the tiles and the short wall mirror the red earth of the surrounding Southwest landscape. This design was planned so the natural colors flow outward, yet the design sets the patio apart from the sagebrush.

PAY ATTENTION TO LEGAL REQUIREMENTS

A visit to your local building department will provide you with information that may minimize headaches later. Most communities have local building codes that govern the construction of permanent features like a patio. Building codes may specify materials, the size of patio, and the location and height of fences. Codes also may require inspection of the construction at different stages— especially for excavations and footings. Check with your building department before you draw your plans, and then take the plans back for approval, permits, and an inspection schedule.

AN EASY WAY TO START

Use existing maps of your property. You can save time and achieve a more accurate base map of your house and property if you start with the existing legal maps and description of your house and lot. These documents—called deed maps, house plans, plat plans, or contour plans—are typically available from your title company, bank, mortgage lender, city hall, or county recorder's office. You may even have a copy in your records. Plot maps do not, however, show every measurement. You'll still have to measure the dimensions of your house and the elements outlined on page 38.

STRUCTURAL ELEMENTS

PLANNING CHECKLIST

Effective patio planning is more than simply drawing and laying a slab or paving materials. A good plan should take into account the details of the total environment. When you are sketching your plans, it's easy to overlook details that you'll later find important. Here's a checklist for the elements to include while you're sketching your patio site. Use the list as a guide. Many items may not apply, and you will add other items specific to your needs.

STRUCTURES
- Dimensions of house, garage, and any other permanent buildings
- Roof overhangs
  Walls, fences, and trellises
- Columns
- Built-in furnishings and appliances (benches, tables, grills, counters)

PAVED SURFACES
- Existing and proposed patio pavings
- Driveways
- Walkways and paths
  Steps
  Edging

AMENITIES (DECORATIVE AND FUNCTIONAL)
- Freestanding furniture and grills
- Lighting
- Play areas
- Poolside areas
- Birdhouses
- Wind chimes
  Sculpture and decorative elements

ACCESS
- Foot traffic patterns
  Doors and windows

DRAINAGE
  Spouts
  Gutters
- Current runoff areas and patterns

SLOPES OR STEEP GRADES
- Dips in ground
- Slope direction
- Steep grades that may need retaining walls
- Stairs and steps

PLACEMENT OF UTILITIES
- Electrical supply lines, overhead or underground
- Telephone lines, overhead or underground
- Television cable
- Natural gas supply lines
- Water supply pipes
- Wastewater pipes
- Hose bibs
- Sewage pipes and catch basins
- Septic tanks
- Utility easements (access for utilities)

PRIVACY AND VIEW
- Open and closed areas within your property
- Views to preserve
- Views to block
- Privacy walls, fences, plants

PLANTS (EXISTING AND PROPOSED)
- Trees
- Shrubs and bushes
- Ground cover
- Ground-level flower beds
- Raised flower beds
- Vegetable or herb gardens
- Edging

WATER AND ROCK
- Erosion
- Natural ponds
- Streams
- Constructed pools and fountains
- Boulders or rock outcroppings

CLIMATE AND MICROCLIMATE
- Prevailing winds
- Precipitation
- Sun and shade
- Heating and cooling

Thanks to careful planning, all the elements of this patio are natural extensions of the landscape. The patio surface is a small raised platform with a bench and a shade structure overhead. The gentle arch of the bridge offsets the rectangular shapes of the decking and overhead.

DRAWING YOUR PATIO

Once you've finished touring, sketching, and measuring your property, it's time to draw an accurate base map. This carefully measured drawing on graph paper will serve as the basis for all of your intermediate and final plans. You will use tracing paper over your base map to experiment with ideas as your plan develops.

BASE MAP

Using 24"×36" graph paper, and with your sketches as a guide, carefully redraw the structural and surface elements of your property to scale. Draw everything to a scale of ¼ inch=1 foot. Show the dimensions of all structures as well as distances from property lines and between structures.

You won't need to put all the items from the checklist (*see page 38*) on your base map, but when you finish, you should have at least the following elements:
- Boundaries
- House and other structures
- Doors, windows, and drains
- Drainage areas
- Existing pavement, walkways, and steps
- Walls and fences
- Garden areas
- Trees and shrubs
- Utilities and easements

BUBBLE PLAN

Tape a sheet of tracing paper over the base map and use a pencil to make circled areas ("bubbles") for specific uses.

For example, you might want to circle one area for eating, another for reading, one for children's play, and another for gardening.

Don't draw specific items like swing sets or barbeques—just circle the areas and label them. If something doesn't work (the dining area is too far away from the kitchen, for example), erase and move it or start another sheet of tracing paper. As you work, refer to your notes about shade patterns, wind flow, and other environmental concerns. Keep experimenting until the layout is functional and incorporates stylistic elements you want.

When the design is right, add bubbles that show problems you want to fix (a privacy fence here, or a drainage system behind the retaining wall). Keep each set of concerns on a single sheet if you can or use separate sheets if things get too cluttered. Add paths, steps, and the raised beds that will complete your bubble plan. Draw arrows to indicate drainage flow, wind currents, and the patterns of normal household traffic. No one is going to criticize your art work at this stage: The goal of bubble plans is to help you consider and organize the possibilities.

DESIGN, DRAFTING, AND MEASURING TOOLS

When you first begin to explore and measure your property, you'll need just a few basic tools—a clipboard, sharpened pencils with erasers, and two good tape measures: one 25 to 30 feet long with a ¾-inch tape and a locking mechanism, and the other 100 feet long.

DRAFTING TOOLS FOR PLANNING: When you're ready to create a base map and finished plan, use a drafting table or other table with 90-degree corners, a T-square, triangle, 24×36" sheets of graph paper with ¼-inch rules, several large sheets of tracing paper, and masking tape to hold the paper in place as you draw. Circle-drawing tools and colored pencils also are handy.

To measure the rise of a short slope use a carpenter's level, a long 2×4, and a measuring tape. A water level also is useful, and you'll need a helper. To find level on steep slopes, widely varying ground levels, or any large surface area with a pronounced slope, rent a professional surveyor's level (also called a transit). This tool lets you work from a single point of reference to consistently gauge heights and slopes throughout the lot. It's easier to use and more accurate than a carpenter's level, and will help ensure that any retaining or decorative walls you build will be even and level at the top. You'll need a helper for a transit, too.

COMPUTER DESIGN AND DRAFTING TOOLS: If you have a home computer, you may find it pays to invest in design and drafting software. While professional programs can cost hundreds of dollars or more, an increasing number of programs for homeowner use are available at a reasonable cost. These programs make it easy to experiment with ideas (the delete function of a computer—an electronic eraser—is a wonderful time-saver) and they are highly accurate tools for placing the design elements. They'll also let you change your mind. Check recent issues of home-improvement magazines for reviews of the newest software. Many home centers and materials suppliers also have computers with design software for customer use.

THE FINAL SKETCH

Now it's time for detail. When you're satisfied that the bubble plan shows where you want things to be on your patio, get a fresh sheet of tracing paper. Carefully draw the details you plan to incorporate into your finished patio. Now you can show the furniture, fireplace, planting boxes, jungle gym, and outdoor lighting. Note dimensions where they're important, and label the different materials (flagstone paving, brick or timber edging, crushed stone on the garden walk).

Show side views of construction details broken out of the plan—the excavation with gravel, concrete pad, and forms.

BUBBLE PLAN

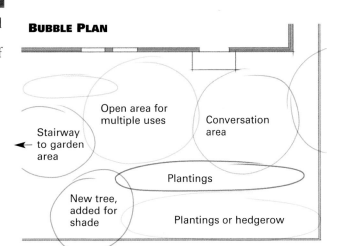

Open area for multiple uses

Conversation area

Stairway to garden area

Plantings

New tree, added for shade

Plantings or hedgerow

Your early sketches need to be useful, not necessarily pretty. Save yourself time and effort at first by keeping things simple. Concentrate on getting the proportions accurate, then focus on how you want to use the space. Once you've figured those things out, you can add more detail. These later drawings can serve as guides while you build.

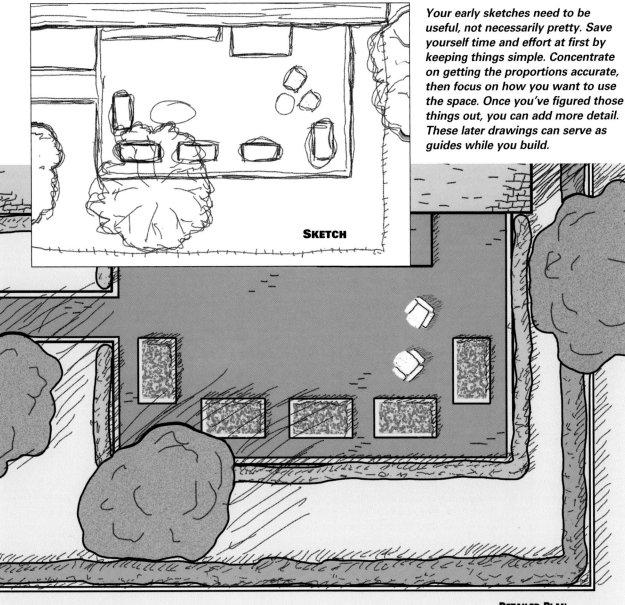

SKETCH

DETAILED PLAN

PUTTING IT TOGETHER

You're ready! With plans in hand, you're prepared to move on to the construction of your new patio.

This chapter guides you through each step of the building process, from groundbreaking to grounded wiring. The principles described here apply to projects of any size, so you can adjust specifications to match your needs. For unusual situations or unique ideas, check with a landscaping specialist before you build—patio projects are time-consuming; you won't want to take apart your work to correct it later.

One prevailing instruction: Take things slowly. You'll be safer and your patio will be better if you don't rush. Here are additional tips to help the job go smoothly:

- *Protect yourself with work clothes, gloves, and boots.*
- *Enlist the help of a friend.*
- *Wear back supports when you lift heavy materials and eye protection when you cut materials that could shatter.*
- *Use a dust mask while you pour dry substances, such as concrete mix or pea gravel.*
- *Work carefully; you'll be finished soon enough.*

WHERE DOES THE TIME GO?

Building a patio often takes more time and effort than you first think it will. There may be more soil to remove than you anticipate or excavation and other tasks you planned to carry out with your own tools that require specialized equipment. For that matter, you might not have thought about how long it really takes to set hundreds of bricks one at a time.

Unlike most other projects, though, building a patio will probably not severely disrupt your daily life. Take advantage of this fact by slowing down and working methodically. You can review and revise your plans as you go along, and you're less likely to injure yourself if you don't hurry. You may be eager to finish the project so that you can relax and enjoy it, but you also can enjoy the work now by slowing down.

Building a patio, even a small one, is a big job—and the job gets even bigger with large areas and ambitious designs. If you have doubts about your ability to construct your own, find a contractor who's willing to let you carry out some of the work. You'll get a reduced price, access to top-quality tools, and advice. In addition, you'll learn new skills and will still be able to put your personal mark on your project.

PREPARING THE FOUNDATION

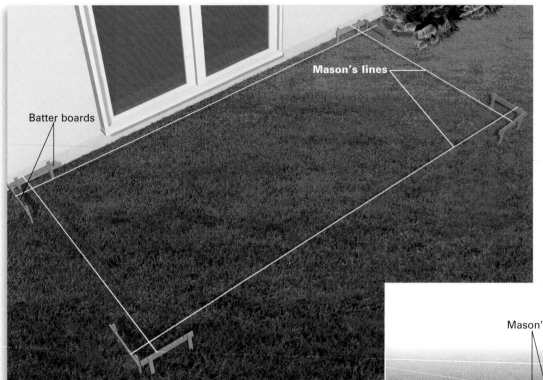

Batter boards

Mason's lines

Make batter boards (below) from scrap wood. Place the batter boards beyond the corners of the patio site (left). Attach mason's lines to the batter boards with nails or wood screws so that you can square the corners.

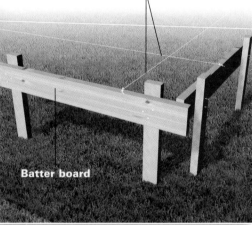

Mason's lines

Batter board

TOOLS YOU'LL NEED

To prepare a building site, you will need tools for leveling and excavation. You may already own most of them. Others are inexpensive, can be rented, or are easy to make from common materials.

■ To check the site for level, use a line level on a mason's line or a water level (you can get one at your hardware store).
■ To check for level over long distances, use a transit (sight level) mounted on a tripod.
■ To mark the edges and measurements of the building site, use brightly colored mason's line.
■ Make stakes and batter boards (to hold the mason's line) from scrap pieces of 1×4 or 2×4 lumber.
■ To transfer measurements from the mason's strings to the ground below, use a plumb bob.
■ For removing sod and soil, use a flat-nosed shovel.
■ To even out rough spots in the excavated surface without gouging, use a garden rake.

You'll need other tools for pouring foundation, and for working with concrete, brick, or tile.

The first step in constructing your patio is to mark the outside edges of the site. Use mason's lines and batter boards to make guides for the edges of your patio. Before you lay out and excavate your patio, you will need to be certain of two things: its dimensions and how you will finish it. Brick and stone can be set in sand or on a concrete base. Soft materials need only a sand base. The excavation depth is different for each surface (*see "Excavation Depths," page 47*) for information about depths for materials.

MAKING BATTER BOARDS

Cut scrap 2×4 lumber to 2-foot lengths, and point the ends so you can drive them into the ground. Fasten a 15- to 18-inch crosspiece to the legs a couple of inches below the tops.

The crosspiece will let you move the mason's line so you can position it where you need it.

Drive batter boards at right angles to each other, 18 to 24 inches beyond the proposed corners of your patio. Don't worry if they're not level; that comes later. Now you're ready for the mason's line.

RUNNING MASON'S LINE

Tie one end of a mason's line to a nail driven roughly in the center of the crosspiece, run the line across to the opposite corner, and fasten it. Repeat the installation of the lines between the remaining batter boards. This is the outside edge of the patio. If your edging is wide (timbers or concrete, for example), a parallel set of lines inside the first set will help you mark the excavation width for the edging.

Now you can level them. Hang a line level (a small, lightweight plastic level with hooks at each end, made especially for this purpose) in the middle of one of the mason's lines, and adjust the height of the line until the bubble in the level is centered between its marks. Adjust the height of the line by driving in the batter boards or by repositioning the mason's line on the crosspiece.

Once you're confident that the first line is level, tighten the line at both ends so that it won't slip. Repeat the leveling procedure until you have all lines level with each other.

To achieve slope for drainage (about 2 percent will do), lower the lines at the outside corners by 1 inch for every 4 running feet. That may seem like undoing what you've already done, but the lines need to be level first so you have a point from which to start.

SQUARING THE CORNERS

Squaring the intersection of the mason's lines requires a little (but simple) geometry called the 3-4-5 method. From each intersection, measure out 3 feet along one line and mark the point with a small piece of masking tape. Measure out 4 feet on the intersecting line and mark it also. Now measure the distance between your tape markers. If it's not exactly 5 feet, move the lines on the crosspieces. When the distance measures 5 feet, your corners are square. Check by measuring the diagonals. The lengths should be equal.

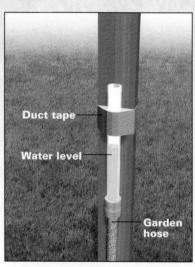

PUT GRAVITY TO WORK

Over long distances, the weight of a line level will put a sag in a mason's line. In such a situation, use a water level (available at your hardware store) instead. Attach the clear plastic to both ends of an almost full hose and fasten the ends to the batter board crosspieces or to stakes. Fill the hose with water until it's visible in the level. Set your batter boards level with this mark.

Duct tape

Water level

Garden hose

Batter board

4'

3'

5'

Over long distances, you can double or triple the 3-4-5 method for squaring corners, marking the lines at 6-8-10 feet, or 9-12-15. Longer measurements will increase the accuracy.

PREPARING THE FOUNDATION
continued

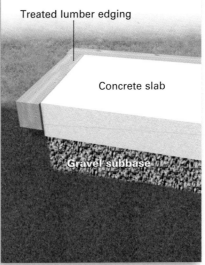

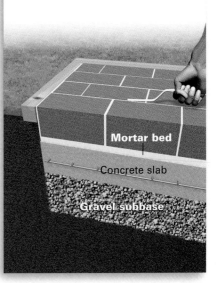

Bricks set in sand or dry mortar form a stable patio surface that flexes with changes in the weather. Installation and repairs also are easy.

A concrete slab is functional and can be colored or patterned with forms to look like flagstone or brick.

For the most permanent brick patio, set brick (or stone) in a mortar bed over a concrete slab.

MARKING THE CORNERS AND EDGES: To mark the corners and edges of the site to know exactly where to dig, attach a length of mason's line to a plumb bob and hang the plumb bob so that the line just touches the intersection of the mason's lines. The point on the ground below the intersection of those lines will become the corner of the excavation. Mark the point with a stake. Plumb and stake each corner and tie a line at ground level tightly between them. Repeat the procedure for the second set of lines (for the edging) if you've installed them. This will give you lines on the ground to dig the edges of your patio. Check your ground line at intervals. Then, mark the ground line with spray paint (get upside down paint at your hardware store—it sprays when the can is inverted) or with powdered chalk from a squeeze bottle. The chalk comes in colors, so you can find one that stands out from the ground color. With the painted or chalked line on the ground, you have a clean edge to start your excavation.

FLAG THE LINES

During the planning stages of your patio project, make a call to all public and private utilities that may have lines on your property. Some also may have easements that require you to provide access on request. Most utilities will locate their lines with marker flags at no cost to their customers.

MAKING CURVED LINES: How do you mark the outline of your patio if the contours are curved? Lay a rope or hose in the shape of the contour—or rounded corners—and mark the line with paint or chalk.

BREAKING GROUND

This is the moment when all your planning suddenly becomes real. Using a square-end spade (or a rented sod cutter, if your patio is large), cut into the ground at the chalked or painted line all the way around the edges, and remove a foot-wide area of sod and soil. Dig carefully to avoid moving the mason's lines and batter boards.

If you plan to save the sod for use in other parts of your landscape, dig it out at an angle in foot-wide strips—at a 2-inch depth to keep the roots intact. Push the shovel handle down sharply to dislodge the roots. When you have the sod strip out, roll it and store it in the shade if you're not going to use it right away.

Excavate the trench for your edging so the edging will be at the height of the finished patio surface. Then excavate another trench along the patio perimeter to the depth required for the material you've chosen. (*see "Excavation Depths," opposite*). Excavating the depth short by an inch or so will raise your patio surface slightly above grade—it makes for easier mowing. Measure the depth from the bottom of the trench to the mason's lines

Grid lines help establish a consistent excavation depth

above. Once the trench is at the right level, stake crosslines every 3 to 4 feet to use as reference points as you dig the rest of the sod and soil.

TYING GRID LINES

Grid lines tied every 4 to 5 feet will give you points to measure your sloped excavation depth. Set stakes (as tall as your batter boards when driven in the ground) at intervals outside the marked excavation line. Tie lines across the patio area so they just touch the lines that are tied to the batter boards. The grid lines will now follow the slope you've set. You can measure at any point on any line to get the correct depth.

Dispense with the crosslines at this point. Excavate and use a carpenter's level on a sloped 2×4 to guide you, or install the grid lines after completing most of the excavation. Using grid lines is more accurate, especially on patios larger than 10×10 feet. You also can install the grid lines before laying sand for a dry-set surface and get the correct slope with the bedding material. For more information about drainage, see pages 48-49.

CLEARING OUT: To clear the remainder of the excavation, stand in the interior and work toward the center, digging toward the trench.

Hold the shovel at a low angle to avoid digging too deep, and remove the surface in small amounts. Excavate the entire area until it's slightly higher than the bottom of the perimeter trench, then measure down from the crosslines. The final surface doesn't have to be perfect; bedding materials will even out small variations. Do not use the ground surface as a reference point—it will rarely be level. Moisten the soil and tamp it with a rented tamper.

Leave the batter boards in place while you excavate the outside edge. Once you've excavated the perimeter, tie grid lines and measure down from them to make the slope of your excavation consistent.

EXCAVATION DEPTHS

How deep you dig will depend on the materials you're using.

DRY-SET BRICK OR STONE: 4 inches of gravel, 2 inches of sand, plus brick or stone thickness.

MORTARED BRICK OR STONE: 4 inches of gravel, 4 inches of concrete, ½ to 1 inch mortar bed, plus surface thickness.

CONCRETE SLAB: 4 inches of gravel plus 4 inches of concrete.

LOOSE MATERIALS: 6 inches (2 inches of sand plus 4 inches of material).

PREPARING THE FOUNDATION
continued

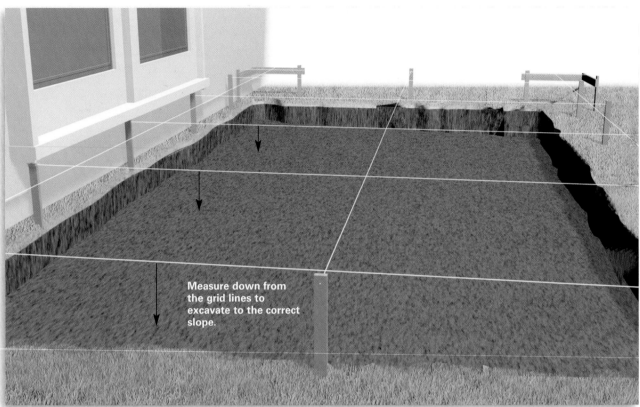

Measure down from the grid lines to excavate to the correct slope.

Your patio should slope at the rate of 1 inch for every 4 running feet. You can slope the mason's lines and dig to a consistent depth, or keep the lines level and dig to the slope.

SLOPING AWAY

Patios next to a houses or other permanent structures should have gentle slopes (about 2 percent, or an inch for every 4 feet) that draw rainwater and melting snow away from the structure. Detached patios also need to be sloped for drainage to prevent water from collecting in low spots or pooling near the edges.

Drainage not only protects your property from erosion, but also makes your patio usable sooner after a rainfall and reduces the chances of ice building up on walking surfaces.

HOW MUCH SLOPE: In general, the patio surface should drop an inch for every 4 feet of horizontal distance. You can create this slope when you excavate the site, but you may find it easier when you install the bedding materials.

CHECKING MEASUREMENTS: Once the bedding materials are laid and smoothed, you should make a final check for slope.

Stand at the higher end of the patio. Measure from the mason's lines to the grade of the bedding material. Next, measure at 4-foot intervals. If you've sloped the mason's lines, the measurements should be the same. If you've left the lines level, the

measurements should be an inch lower every 4 feet (*see pages 51 and 57 for more information about bedding installation*).

DRAINAGE OPTIONS

Achieving proper drainage in moderately wet climates is a simple matter of creating a sloped surface with sloped bedding materials. If your region has unusually high amounts of precipitation, however, or if the water table is unusually high, subsurface moisture and spring snowmelt can be trapped, and freezes can heave and crack the surface. Patios built on clay soil (which does not drain well) or at the base of steep hills also are subject to drainage problems. If your site is situated in any of these conditions, add additional drainage systems.

SWALES: Swales are shallow trenches (about 4 inches deep) that intercept and redirect water. A swale can be planted with grass or lined with tile and extended under structures with drain pipe. A swale planted with grass will slow the water flow and let the ground absorb it—preferable to emptying onto open ground. Be sure your swale doesn't send water into your neighbor's yard—that's illegal.

OPTIONS FOR DRAINAGE

A dry well collects water that drains from the patio through a 4-inch perforated drainpipe. A hole 3 feet deep and 3 feet wide should be large enough for most locations. Fill the hole with gravel, and place a layer of landscaping fabric over the surface to prevent soil from plugging the gravel.

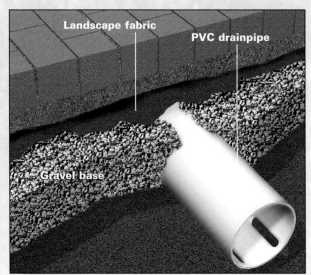

A perforated drainpipe set just under the patio surface directs accumulating water away from the patio subsurface. Coarse gravel around the pipe lets the water flow into the pipe, and landscape fabric keeps weeds down and prevents soil from washing into the gravel and drainpipe.

In some locations, grading alone is not enough to provide adequate drainage. Here are three options for improving the speed and volume of drainage. Once they are built, they are virtually maintenance free.

DRY WELL: A dry well is a large, gravel-filled hole located at a spot lower than the patio (but above the water table) and removed from the patio site. A dry well collects water and lets it slowly disperse into the surrounding soil. It must be connected to the site by drainpipe sloped 1 inch every 4 feet. Dig a hole 3 feet deep and 2 to 4 feet wide. Fill it with coarse gravel, cover the gravel with landscape fabric, then topsoil and sod. Landscape fabric keeps soil from washing into the gravel.

DRAINAGE TRENCHES: Dig drainage trenches either around the perimeter or underneath the surface. Subsurface trench depth varies with climate; check with a landscape expert to get the right depth. Perimeter drains should be 4 inches deep and set with a concrete channel. In both cases, the trenches should slope 1 inch every 4 feet. Line the recess of either drain with gravel and then install perforated drainpipe, keeping the slope consistent. Cover the pipe with more gravel, landscape fabric, and then the patio bedding.

CATCH BASIN: A catch basin is an open surface drain with a receptacle that holds water and disperses it through piping when it reaches a certain level. Dig a hole at the lowest point of the patio so the patio surface drains toward it. The hole should be wide enough to accommodate the prefab catch basin (available at garden centers) and deeper by 4 inches (for a gravel base). Dig a trench for the outlet pipe and slope the pipe to a distant dry well or—if codes permit—to the storm sewer system in your area.

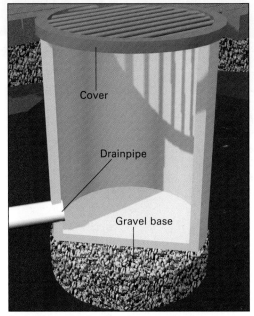

Install a catch basin where patio sites are too low to drain. A catch basin gives the water somewhere to go. Concrete catch basins are sold ready to install. Place one at the lowest point of your site, but within the patio area. The drainpipe can empty into a distant dry well or—if local codes allow—into the storm sewer system.

PREPARING THE FOUNDATION
continued

Tamp small areas by hand. If you don't own a hand tamper, make one from a 4×4 and a 10-inch square plate of ¾-inch plywood.

A power tamper will compress the soil and subbase materials more quickly and completely than can be done by hand. You also should use a power tamper for packing sand in dry-set installations.

TAMPING

Once the site is excavated, remove roots and rocks. Next, compact the soil to reduce ground settling and to provide a firm base for the bedding materials. Rent a power tamper for any area larger than 10 square feet; hand tamping is strenuous and produces inconsistent results on large areas.

EDGING

If you're pouring concrete, now is the time to install forms along the edges; however, vertical brick edging goes in after excavation. For other edging materials, it's also usually easier to install the edging now. It will help you guide the screeding (leveling) of the subbase materials.

Edging defines the perimeter of the patio, contains loose materials, and should be an integral part of the design. Depending on the surface material, edging can be strictly functional, such as 2×4 forms for poured concrete, or decorative.

BRICK EDGING: One of the oldest edging designs involves using the same material on both the patio surface and around the border. Almost any brick pattern can be edged with the same bricks set with a different method. Set bricks on end to create a consistent border of small shapes. Brick used to edge a concrete slab adds an effective contrast, especially to patterned concrete.

CONCRETE EDGING: Although most people don't think of concrete as attractive, it provides a strong and—if colored or stamped—unusual edge for any paving material. Poured in forms to take any shape, concrete also can serve as the base for brick or stone edging set in mortar. Make forms from 2× stock whose width will bring the edging level with the patio surface. Drive stakes behind the forms and tie the tops of the forms with 1× stock every 4 feet—to keep them from bowing.

PLASTIC EDGING: Popular and widely available, plastic edging costs relatively little and withstands any climate without damage from exposure to sunlight, water, or severe weather. It can be laid out below the ground to keep pavers from shifting, or above the ground as a decorative border. Plastic edgers are held in place with 10-inch spikes. They

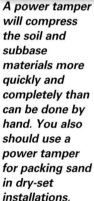

WORTH RENTING

A gas-powered tamper may seem like an unnecessary expense. A homemade tamper is easy enough to build and use, so why spend more money on a rental tool? Results, that's why. A gas-powered tamper works effectively and quickly, which saves you time and effort, and will help you create a patio bed that is far less likely to sink or shift over time.

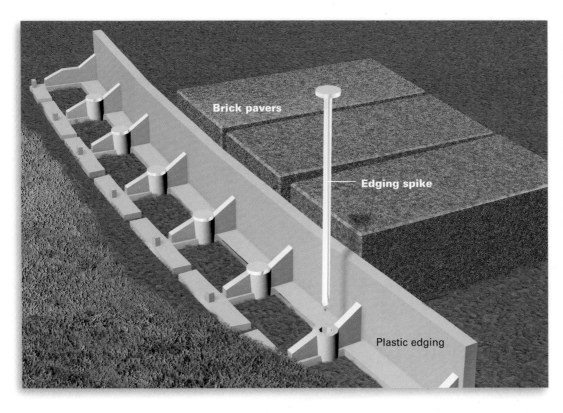

Brick pavers

Edging spike

Plastic edging

Plastic edging, available at most building supply stores, keeps loose pavers aligned at the borders of the patio. Cover it with soil after the pavers are in place to create an invisible edge. Use plenty of edging spikes.

are rigid enough to support paving materials, and flexible enough to be worked into curves.

WOOD EDGING: Set pressure-treated or redwood landscape timbers in a trench around your patio site to contain pavers, concrete, or loose fill. Predrill the timbers and drive spikes through the holes into the ground. Railroad ties add a more massive look. For a less visible border, set 1× pressure-treated stock rated for ground contact against the outside edge of the trench to hold loose fill. Or use wooden forms and stakes set below ground level. Staked benderboard holds poured concrete slabs to almost any curved shape.

PUTTING IN THE BED

Loose materials require only a 2-inch sand base. All other patio surfaces need a 4-inch bed of gravel as their base to provide a solid foundation and good drainage. What goes on top of the gravel depends on how the patio will be finished. Brick, stone, and concrete pavers set in sand will get a 2-inch sand base over the gravel (lay landscape fabric first to keep the weeds out). So will dry-mortared finishes. Mortared surfaces call for a 4-inch concrete slab. You won't need landscape fabric for mortared surfaces.

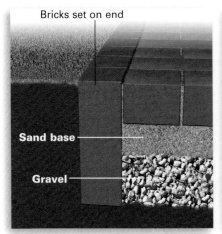

Bricks set on end

Sand base

Gravel

Bricks set on end, called "soldiers" or "sailors," form a simple border using the same material as the surface.

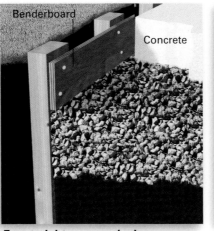

Benderboard

Concrete

For straight or curved edges on a concrete slab, use benderboard (thin plywood) held in place with stakes.

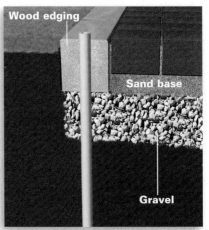

Wood edging

Sand base

Gravel

A galvanized steel pipe can serve as a stake for pressure-treated wood edging. Predrill the edging first.

BUILDING A BRICK-IN-SAND PATIO

To hold brick pavers in place invisibly, stake plastic edging along the border so that the lower edges of the brick will be held by the plastic (right). Cover the edging with dirt or loose fill. For a decorative edge, set bricks on end: standing up straight or at an angle (below).

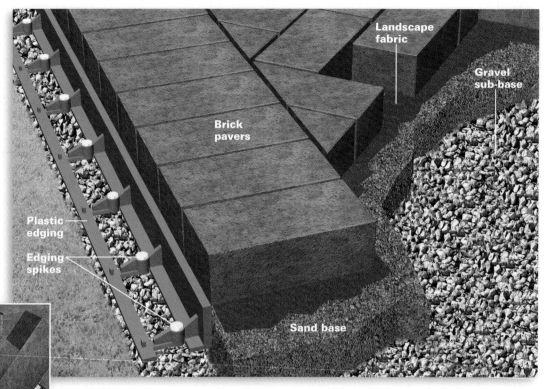

Landscape fabric

Gravel sub-base

Brick pavers

Plastic edging

Edging spikes

Sand base

A patio made of bricks set in sand is one the easiest outdoor projects to start, install, and finish. You don't have to worry about mortar setting up, so you can lay part of it on one weekend and finish up the next.

EXCAVATION

Before you lay out the site, compute the dimensions so that you will minimize the number of cut brick. Divide the dimensions by the *actual* size of the brick you've chosen, allowing for ⅛-inch gaps between them.

Then lay out and excavate the site, using the methods discussed on pages 44–51. The excavation should be deep enough for a 4-inch gravel base, a 2-inch sand bed, and the thickness of the brick (2 to 3 inches). Subtract 1 inch if you want the surface to be slightly higher than grade—the raised edge makes mowing easier. Allow for slope, and tamp the soil with a rented power tamper.

INSTALLING THE EDGING

Installation techniques for edging vary with the kind of edge you want to create.

■ **BRICK SOLDIERS AND SAILORS:**
Soldiers are set on end with the widest side facing the patio surface. Sailors have the narrow side facing the surface. Either way, set them in before you pour the gravel.

■ **BRICK OR STONE IN CONCRETE:**
If the edging will be set in concrete, dig a trench wide enough for forms. Use staked 2× stock with the top at the same level as the finished patio. Pour the concrete and let it cure for at least three days. Mortar the surface and install the edge material. Let the mortar cure for two days before removing the forms.

■ **TIMBER EDGING:** If you're installing timber edging, dig the trench now—out from the perimeter and slightly wider than the timbers. Install the timbers, backfill behind them, and drive spikes into the ground though predrilled holes.

■ **PLASTIC EDGING:** Set rigid plastic edging in a trench and hold it in place with metal spikes. The top ridge of the edging should extend above the sand base by about half the thickness of the pavers.

■ **TEMPORARY GUIDES:** If you're using edging that you will install after the paving is laid, install temporary screed guides (2× stock staked and even with the finished surface).

SETTING THE BASE

■ Before you lay in gravel, set stakes at various locations in the bed, driving them in so the tops are 4 inches above the surface.
■ Shovel in the gravel even with the stakes

and rake it roughly level with a garden rake.

■ Set a long, straight 2×4 at an angle on the surface of the subbase to smooth it. Fill in low spots and rake away gravel from high spots until the surface is consistent over the entire site and slopes properly for drainage. When the surface of the subbase is uniform, and meets the 4-inch marks on the stakes, compact the gravel with a tamper.

■ To prevent weeds and grass from growing through the subbase, lay down a layer of landscaping fabric before pouring the sand base. Overlap fabric joints by at least one foot.

Shovel washed sand into the site and spread it evenly with a garden rake. At various locations, push a stake or rod—marked at 2 inches—into the sand. Push the sand into all the edges and corners until the surface is relatively uniform.

SCREEDING

Screeding is leveling. To make a screed, use a 2×6 long enough to span the patio and cut out the ends. The cutouts should be wide enough to ride on the edging or temporary guides and deep enough to level the sand at the thickness of your brick.

■ Pull the screed slowly across the entire surface of the sand base, working it from side to side as you pull it.

■ Soak the sand base thoroughly with a garden hose nozzle set to fine mist. Compact the wet sand with a tamper.

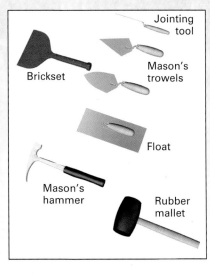

WORKING WITH BRICK

Jointing tool

Mason's trowels

Brickset

Float

Mason's hammer

Rubber mallet

Compared to other paving materials, bricks are relatively easy to cut, handle, and install. The work is even easier if you have the right tools. Some tools are available from the brick supplier; you should be able to find others you need at any large building supply store.

■ To cut individual bricks to special sizes or shapes, use a chisel called a brickset.

■ For driving the brickset, use a mason's hammer (the chiseled end is for trimming cuts).

■ For tapping bricks in sand or dry mortar without damaging them, use a rubber mallet.

■ To apply wet mortar to the surfaces of brick, use a mason's trowel—use the handle to tap them in place.

■ To finish the surface of mortar joints, called striking, use a convex jointer or V-jointer.

■ Any time you cut brick, you may knock sharp fragments loose.

■ Be sure to wear eye protection and a dust mask if sawing.

■ To finish the surface of a concrete slab, use a float.

Beveled stakes

Screed

Forms

Stakes

Level the sand base with a notched 2×6 for a screed board. To keep the screed board from catching on the stakes, bevel them (above) or set them below the forms (left).

BUILDING A BRICK-IN-SAND PATIO
continued

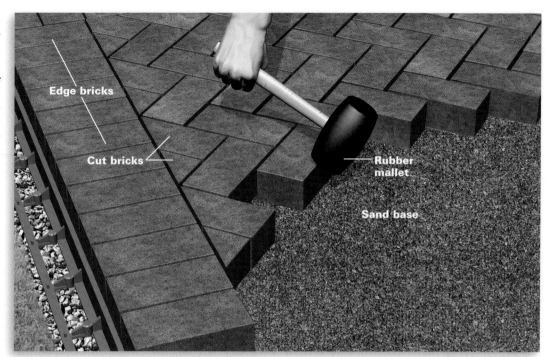

Place each brick by hand, and give it a gentle tap with a rubber mallet if necessary to make it fit. Add or remove small amounts of sand to get each brick level with the others.

Edge bricks

Cut bricks

Rubber mallet

Sand base

Check for level with mason's lines or with a carpenter's level on the surface.

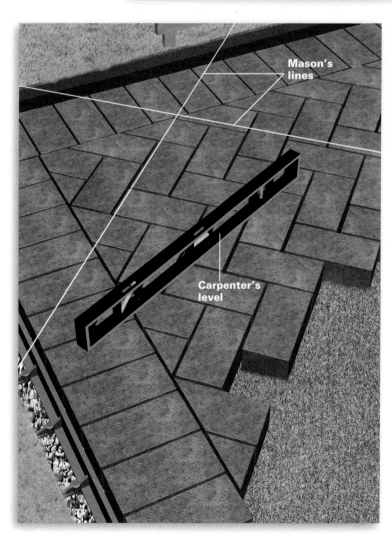

Mason's lines

Carpenter's level

■ Fill in low spots with more sand, then wet and tamp again. Continue adding sand, tamping, and leveling with the screed board until the sand is uniformly 2 inches deep and the surface is consistent across the entire site.

SETTING BRICKS

Before you start laying the pattern, take a trial run. Lay out a small section, beginning in the corners and extending far enough to give you an idea of how often the pattern calls for cut brick.

Now remove the trial brick and start laying them in the corners—this time for real. If you use plastic edging, the outer row should fit snugly against the plastic. For other edging, leave a ⅛-inch gap (use plastic spacers or plywood). You can keep the lines straight by tying mason's line to bricks and stretching it across the surface.
■ Set bricks by pushing straight down— don't slide them—then tap them in place with a rubber mallet.
■ Lay out the pattern in all directions outward from the corner. Tap each brick into place with the mallet to make sure the surfaces match.
■ Every three or four rows, lay a carpenter's level and sloping jig across the surface of the pavers to check your progress. (Cut a 2×4 to the angle of the slope and set the carpenter's level on it to make the level read accurately). If the surface is low in some places, remove

METHODS OF CUTTING BRICK

To cut brick with a brickset, first place the brick on a board. Score the brick lightly on all sides to create a cut line, then strike the chisel with greater force. Wear safety goggles.

You also can cut brick with a circular saw and masonry blade. Saw cuts are more accurate than chisel cuts and more consistent. Wear goggles and a dust mask.

To remove a small bump from the face of a cut brick, strike the bump sharply with the edge of a mason's trowel or with the chisel end of a bricklayer's hammer.

Once all the bricks are in place, shovel a pile of clean, dry sand on the surface and distribute it with a push broom. Sweep from all directions to push the sand into the joints.

the pavers, add more sand, tamp, and replace the pavers. If some spots are a bit high, you can adjust the paver height with a few sharp taps from the mallet, or scrape out sand and replace the paver.

FILLING GAPS

Sprinkle sand over the entire surface of the patio and sweep it back and forth into the joints with a push broom. Make sure you sweep from all directions. When the joints are full, sweep the excess to one side (or collect it) and settle the sand with a fine mist from the garden hose. Continue sweeping sand and settling it until the joints are full. Then tamp the surface with a power tamper.

SETTING BRICKS IN DRY MORTAR

To make the pavers stay in place more securely, fill the joints with dry mortar and sand (1 part portland cement to 4 parts sand). Lay pavers with a ½-inch gap. Sweep the sand-and-cement mixture over the pavers, then tamp it with a ½-inch board. Add dry mix until the joints are full, then spray the surface with a fine mist of water. When the mortar will retain a thumbprint, tool it with a jointer. Once it's firm, scrub off the excess.

To help pack the sand in the joints, spray the patio with a fine mist from a garden hose; sweep more sand and spray again.

SETTING BRICK ON A CONCRETE SLAB

Brick on mortar packs a double dose of patio building: You build one patio—the concrete slab—then add the brick surface.

If you already have a sturdy, level slab in place, you're halfway there. Bear in mind, laying brick on an old concrete patio will raise its surface, so you may want to include some additional grading to raise the surrounding landscape.

LAYING OUT A SLAB

To lay out the excavation area for a new slab, start by making sure its dimensions will accommodate your pattern. Most paving brick is 4×8 inches, but some nominally-sized 4×8 pavers are ½- to ⅜-inch less than the stated size. Measure the brick you're using and include the width of the mortar joint when figuring dimensions. Divide the patio dimensions by the "real" brick length and width (brick size plus mortar) and adjust the final size so it will accommodate the pattern.

Next, set temporary stakes at approximate corner locations. Drive a pair of batter boards at right angles to each other about 18 inches beyond the corners. Attach mason's lines to the center of the crosspieces with nails or screws and pull them relatively tight.

Use the 3-4-5 method (see page 45) to square the corners and allow for a slope of 1 inch per 4 running feet (see page 48).

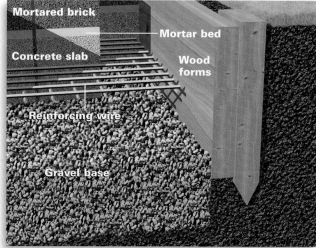

Mortared brick should be set on a 4-inch reinforced concrete slab with a 4-inch gravel base.

Install, square, and slope a second set of lines parallel to the first and as wide as the proposed edging. (Skip this step for narrow edgings—just be sure the single set of mason's lines represents the width of the patio including the edging.)

Drop a plumb bob at the intersection of the lines and drive a stake; these are the real corner points. Run a tight mason's line at ground level for the excavation line. Chalk the ground line or spray it with paint.

EXCAVATING

A concrete slab needs a 4-inch gravel base and the slab itself is 4 inches thick, so your excavation needs to be 8 inches deep, plus the thickness of your brick. Dig it 1 to 2 inches less than the total material thickness so the finished surface will be slightly above grade for easier mowing and to allow for some eventual settling. Start digging about 6 inches outside the excavation line (you'll need the extra room to install forms), and excavate the patio site to a uniform sloped depth (see page 48).

SETTING FORMS

Drive 2×4 stakes at the corners and attach 2×8s for the forms. To keep the forms from bowing, drive 2×4 stakes outside the forms at 2-foot intervals. Attach the forms to the stakes with screws or duplex nails (they have two heads and will pull out easily when you're done). Make sure the forms have the proper slope as you install them—measure down from the sloped mason's lines.

EVALUATING AN OLD SLAB

Look over the existing concrete slab. Is it in the location you want? If it's not large enough, but it's placed where you want it, expand its area with additional concrete.

Now take a close look at its condition. First check its depth and gravel base. Dig down along one side. The gravel base should be 4 inches deep and so should the slab. If the gravel is in good shape but the slab is not thick enough, you can add concrete after roughing and cleaning it.

Next, inspect the surface. Look for deep cracks, places that have sunk or heaved, and large areas that have begun to deteriorate. If any of these conditions exist, it's time to break up the existing slab and start over. The surface can be sloped for drainage, but should be uniform throughout, with no more than a ⅛-inch variance every 10 square feet. Repair minor high spots or flaking by breaking them out with a small sledge and applying a concrete patch. Then roughen the surface with a rented sandblaster or scarifier, or etch it with 1 part muriatic acid and 4 parts water, and wash it with a hard spray from the hose.

PREPARING THE BED

Next, pour in a 4-inch base of gravel, shoveling it tight against the forms. Level the gravel with a screed board (a 2×6 with the ends cut out so they ride along the surface of the forms). Add gravel to low spots and tamp it with a power tamper.

Lay in reinforcing wire mesh (use a gauge that is called 6×6 10/10) supported on and tied to dobies—small 2-inch-thick concrete (not brick) blocks whose job it is to keep the wire mesh centered halfway through concrete when it's poured. Overlap the ends of the mesh by 4 inches and tie them with wire.

POURING THE SLAB

If you pour your own (easy enough on slabs 10×10 or smaller), make a runway for your wheelbarrow with 2×10s. If you use ready-mix, make sure the truck can get as close to the site as possible without damaging your driveway or lawn.

Mix bags of premix in a power mixer and pour it in wheelbarrow loads. Pour the concrete uniformly into the excavation, and work it up and down with a shovel to set it and release air bubbles. Drag a 2×4 (long enough to span the width) to level the concrete with the forms. Fill voids, and level again.

Roughen the surface of the wet concrete with a homemade scarifier—drive nails at 1-inch intervals into an 18-inch 2×2. The grooves made by the nails do not have to be deep—just enough to give the mortar a "tooth" to bind it to the surface. Then let the concrete cure for 3 to 7 days, keeping it moist with burlap (spray it occasionally) or cover it with plastic sheets.

Notched screed board

To create a smooth surface below the tops of the forms, notch a screed board and slide it along the top edges of the forms as you work.

LAYING BRICK

Before you start, reinstall mason's lines at the finished surface of the patio. Then add water to premixed mortar using a mortar box or wheelbarrow. You'll know when you have the mix right when it hangs on the surface of a trowel turned on edge.

Use the trowel handle to tap bricks level into the mortar bed. Make sure the top of the surface is consistent— use a carpenter's level to check it every 6 to 8 square feet.

Spread mortar (type M is for outdoor use) in a ½-inch bed in 4×4-foot sections. Don't spread (or mix) more than you can handle in about an hour. On a hot dry day, mortar will start drying out in as little as 15 minutes.

Start in a corner and work in square or triangular sections, depending on the pattern you have chosen. Push each brick straight down with a firm motion and tap it in place with a rubber mallet. Use ⅜- or ½-inch plywood spacers as you work—the same spacer width you used when you calculated the patio dimensions. Tie mason's line to bricks and set them on line with your pattern to help keep the courses straight.

As you complete each section, lay a 2×4 on the surface. Pull out low pavers, remortar, and reset the brick. Tap down pavers that are high.

When you have laid the entire surface, let the mortar cure for 3 days, then pack the joints with mortar. Use a pointed mason's trowel or, better yet, a mortar bag. The bag has a pointed nozzle to squeeze the mortar into the joints— it's more precise and you'll make less mess. Clean spilled mortar right away with a wet sponge. When the joints will hold a thumb print, finish them with a jointing tool. Keep the surface moist for 3 or 4 days so it cures slowly.

Using the edge of a mason's trowel, add a thin line of mortar to all the joints between the bricks. Take care to avoid getting the mortar on the brick surfaces.

FLAGSTONE PATIO

Because flagstones have uneven surfaces, they often shift or wobble at first. Give them a healthy base in which to set—2 inches of sand, or, as shown here, a 1-inch mortar bed.

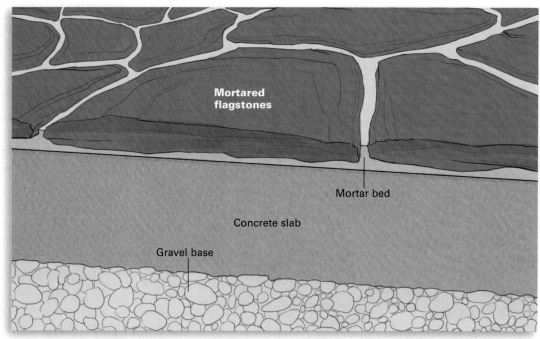

Mortared flagstones

Mortar bed

Concrete slab

Gravel base

The look of flagstone has a timeless appeal, and for good reason. Its rough-hewn, natural look brings a rustic charm to almost any landscape design.

Like brick, you can set flagstone on a sand base or mortar it to a concrete slab. Dry-set surfaces flex and fall back with changes in ground temperatures. Mortared surfaces are solid and need a concrete base to keep them from cracking. Both installations need a gravel subbase for support and drainage.

Installation techniques are almost the same, as discussed below. What's different about setting flagstone is that you can't predict the pattern until you have it on site because it's irregular. Even cut flagstone is not uniformly modular, so you will have to experiment with your design before you actually set it.

To estimate the amount of stone required, figure a ton for every 120 square feet. Draw free-form designs on graph paper and count the number of whole squares to get the area. Order about five percent more for waste.

PREPARING THE SITE

Site layout for both a dry-set or mortared stone patio is the same. But because stone lends itself to more free-flowing designs, you have more layout options than with regular materials.

SQUARE AND RECTANGULAR DESIGNS: Unlike brick installations, stone patios do not have to precisely accommodate modular materials. Figure the dimensions of your patio space—you won't have to make adjustments—but make sure your dimensions include the width of your edging material. Drive temporary corner stakes and set batter boards at right angles about 18 inches beyond

CUTTING STONE

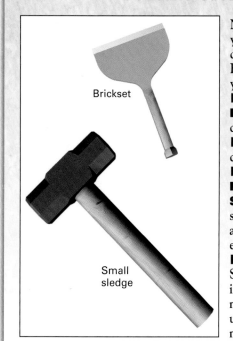

Brickset

Small sledge

No matter what layout you plan, you'll need to cut some of the stones. Here are the basic tools you need:

■ **CARPENTER'S PENCIL:** For marking cut lines on the stone.
■ **BRICKSET:** To score cut lines.
■ **MASON'S HAMMER AND SMALL SLEDGE:** For striking the brickset accurately and with enough force.
■ **SAFETY GOGGLES:** Stone can shatter when it's cut. Wear a dust mask, too, if you're using a saw with a masonry blade.

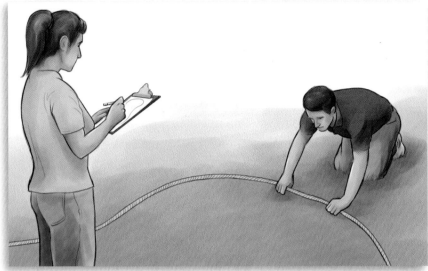

SIZE, SHAPE, AND COLOR

Variety, a design strength of flagstone, also can be a weakness. Because flagstones range in size from skipping stones to carports, you need to plan for sizes that will best fit the scale of your patio project. A variety of sizes will also add versatility to your design.

Shape is another factor that can work in your favor—or not, depending on the amount of time you're willing to spend finding stones that fit together well. A carelessly chosen grouping will look as if they were placed by accident.

Finally, flagstones are available in several colors, sometimes within a single shipment from one supplier. If your design already uses variations in shape and texture, you may not want to add more contrast.

the corners. Fasten mason's lines to the batter board crosspieces with nails (or tie them), square them with the 3-4-5 method (*see page 45*) and slope them for drainage (1 inch every 4 feet). Install a second set of lines to mark the interior of your edging material.

Mark the corners with a stake at the point under the intersecting lines where a plumb bob comes to rest. String mason's lines between the stakes at ground level and pull tight. The ground line marks where to dig. Chalk or paint along the ground line and pull it up.

CONTOURED DESIGNS: To make a free-flowing design or a rectangle combined with curves, stake out the maximum length and width of the patio site. Lay rope within the limits defined by the stakes and experiment until you get the shape you want. Step back from time to time to evaluate the shape. When you're sure the contour is right, chalk the rope or use paint to mark it. Then install batter boards as described above—you won't need them for squaring corners, but you will need them for establishing an excavation that's sloped for correct drainage.

Lay out the shape of the proposed flagstone patio with a rope or garden hose. Step back and look at it from a variety of perspectives. Adjust it until you're happy with the shape, then mark the line with chalk or paint.

EXCAVATING

Excavation for both dry-set and mortared surfaces is the same, but each requires a different depth, and mortared stone will need forms and a concrete slab.

STONE-IN-SAND PATIOS require a depth of 8 to 9 inches (4-inch gravel base, 2-inch sand bed, plus 2 to 3 inches of stone thickness). Subtract 1 to 2 inches from this

Arrange the flagstones on the ground after excavating. You may need to test several variations on your original idea before you find one that looks right. On the lawn nearby, set the flagstones aside in the same arrangement. You won't have time to change your mind once you start spreading the mortar bed.

FLAGSTONE PATIO
continued

MAKING A FLAGSTONE WALK

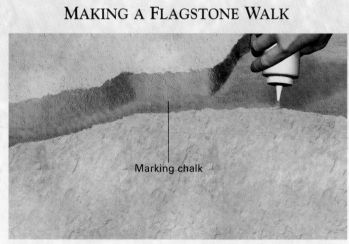

Marking chalk

To make a flagstone walkway, set individual flagstones directly on the ground. Mark around the edge of each stone with chalk to show where you will need to excavate. Set the flagstones aside.

Dig recesses for the flagstones, making each the same depth of the stone that will sit in it. To help the stones settle in place, dig the trenches deeper and add a layer of sand.

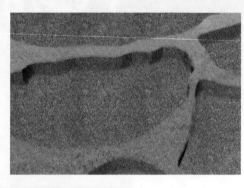

Place each flagstone in the recess dug for it, and move the stone around a bit to push it down. If the stones sit too high in their trenches, dig a bit deeper; if they're too low, add some sand.

The finished result should be a pathway that blends with the surrounding turf. A successful flagstone path should look as if it had always been there.

depth if you want the finished surface to be above grade. Excavate the site, using the methods shown on pages 46-51, and check for slope as you go against perimeter and grid lines. Moisten the soil and power tamp.

MORTARED STONE excavations will need to be 10¼ to 12 inches deep (4 inches gravel, 4 inches concrete pad, ¾ to 1 inch mortar bed and 2 to 3 inches of stone paving). Dig out the site with the proper slope, using mason's and grid lines for reference points. Moisten the soil and tamp it with a power tamper.

FORMS AND EDGING

Although flagstone patios can be edged with the same materials as brick, the irregularity of stone lends itself well to free-form design and hidden edging. Whatever your edging choice, installing it now will give you a consistent reference point for laying the surface level.

DRY-SET SURFACES: Use the methods described for edging a brick patio (*see page 52*), digging trenches for brick, timber, or plastic. You also can set temporary guides for screeding (staked 2× stock whose top edge is flush with the finished surface).

MORTARED STONE SURFACES: Drive 2×4 stakes at the corners of the site and attach 2×8s to them with duplex nails. To keep the forms from bowing, drive 2×4 stakes outside the forms and nail them, also. Measure down from the perimeter mason's lines so the forms conform to the slope for drainage.

MAKING A CONCRETE BASE

GRAVEL BED: Using the methods described above, level a 4-inch gravel base and tamp it even with the tops of 4-inch stakes.

REINFORCEMENT: Lay in reinforcing wire mesh (ask for 6×6 10/10). The mesh will help keep the concrete pad from cracking. Overlap the joints in the mesh by 4 inches and tie them at the joints. Support the mesh and tie it to dobies (small 2-inch concrete block that will center the mesh in the slab).

POURING THE SLAB: If your site is 10×10 or less, mix the concrete from premix bags. For larger sites, order ready-mix. Carry it to the site in wheelbarrow loads (a 2×12 runway will make this easier) and pour it to a 4-inch depth. Work a shovel up and down in the poured mix to get it into recesses and remove air. Span the site with a 2×4 laid on the forms, and work the board back and forth to level the concrete. Roughen the surface with a scarifier (*see page 57*), or notched trowel and let the concrete cure for 3 to 7 days.

Hauling concrete is difficult—more so on uncovered turf. Make a runway from 2×12s so you can move the wheelbarrow with less effort. Enlist the aid of helpers to move and settle the concrete in the forms.

MAKING A DRY-SET BED

GRAVEL BASE: Drive stakes every 4 to 5 square feet so the tops are 4 inches from the excavation surface. Shovel the gravel level with the stakes and spread it with a garden rake. Screed (*see "Screeding," pages 53–54*) the surface or level it with a 2×4, fill in low spots, and tamp with a power tamper. Lay landscape fabric to keep the weeds down.

SAND BED: Shovel washed sand into the site and spread it with a garden rake. Check for a 2-inch thickness and screed with a 2×6 long enough to span the site. Cut out the ends of the screed so they ride on the edging or screed guides at a depth that will level the sand at 2 inches. Work the screed back and forth, moisten the sand, and tamp it. Add sand, moisten, and tamp until the bed is uniform.

TAKING A TEST DRIVE

No two flagstones are the same (not even those cut in rectangles), so you'll need to experiment with the pattern. This may take some time, but you'll be more satisfied with the results if you don't rush the process. You can do this before you excavate, but your dry run will be easier after excavation. Set stones on the surrounding ground so you can see the shapes and sizes. Then lay the pieces out in the bed, using the suggestions on page 62

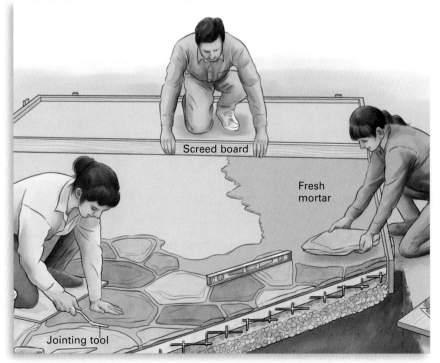

One way to produce a level mortar bed is to screed it—but don't lay in too much mortar at once. Mortar sets up quickly, especially in hot weather. Get others to help, so you can keep things moving.

Screed board

Fresh mortar

Jointing tool

CUTTING FLAGSTONE

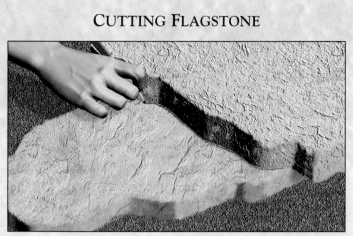

With care and practice, you can cut one flagstone so that it fits well with another. Place the flagstone to be cut underneath the one whose pattern you want to match. Trace the contour of the top stone on the bottom one with a carpenter's pencil, repeating the line until it is easy to see.

Tap the brickset with a sledge or mason's hammer to score the pencil line. The scored line gives the stone a place to fracture when it is cut.

After scoring the contour, set the flagstone on a piece of lumber, with the scoring line placed just past the edge of the board. Hold the larger side steady, and strike the smaller piece sharply with a sledge. The stone will break along the scoring line. Clean up small bumps or ridges on the flagstone with a hammer and chisel or a mason's hammer.

FLAGSTONE PATIO
continued

as a guide. *Note: If you're working on a sand base, support your weight with 3×3 plywood platforms to keep from indenting and dislodging the sand.*

■ Don't treat the stones as individual pieces; see how they look in pairs and threes. Visualize sections, not puzzle pieces. Don't worry about getting the contours to match exactly; flagstones can be cut to fit. Use small stones as corner fillers.

■ Vary the size, shape, and color as you go. Variety is not only the spice of life—it can liven up your patio, too.

■ Keep the spacing as uniform as possible— ½ to ¾ of an inch for both dry-set and mortared surfaces. Use wider, consistent spacing for turf or planted joints.

■ Once the pattern is laid, stand back and look at it from different perspectives. Rearrange it if you don't like it, then leave the stones in place for the final bedding.

SETTING STONES IN SAND

Before adding sand to the joints, place a long 2×4 at several angles across the surface, checking for high and low stones. Use a carpenter's level to check the slope. Pull up high stones, dig out sand to conform to the bottom of the stone, and reset. Add sand and place low stones. Then walk the surface and correct stones that "rock."

Sprinkle washed sand across the entire surface and sweep it into the joints with a push broom. When the joints are full, collect the excess and wet the sand with a fine mist. Continue adding sand and wetting it until the joints are full. Then sweep the surface clean.

You also can fill joints with dry mortar, using the methods described for brick on page 55.

MAKING THE MORTAR BED

To retain the pattern, lift the stones out in 3×3-foot sections—the size of an area you can finish in 10 to 15 minutes. Lay them on the grass next to the site in the same pattern. Mix enough type M mortar (it's for outdoor use) for the section and spread it with a trowel on the surface of the concrete slab— 1 inch thick. Take the stones up from the surrounding grass and reset each one in the mortar bed, being careful to keep the joints at the original spacing. Push the stones down; don't slide them in place. Tap them with a rubber mallet. As you complete each section, lay a 2×4 across it. You are certain to have high and low stones. Fix them now—you

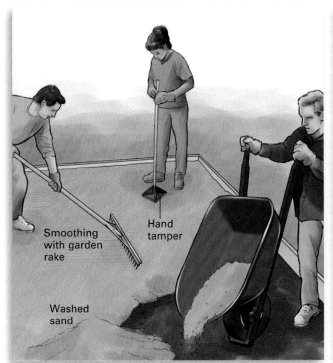

Pour in the sand, smooth it out with a garden rake to distribute it evenly, then tamp it in place. The sand will need to shift a bit to accommodate the flagstones, so you don't need to get it perfect at this point. On small sites, you may be able to get by with a hand tamper; however, a rented power tamper is usually worth the expense.

When you lay out stones for your patio, use larger stones to set the general pattern. You may need to rearrange them several times. Once you have the pattern set, use smaller stones to fill the gaps between the larger ones.

won't be able to later. Pull out stones that are low, add mortar, and reset them. Tap down the high stones, and if necessary, lift them and scoop just enough mortar out to make them level again. Then clean off any spills with a wet broom and set the next and succeeding sections. Let the mortar cure for 3 to 4 days, remove any temporary forms, and then fill the joints.

MORTARING STONE JOINTS

Mix mortar in a mortar box and fill the joints using a pointed trowel or mortar bag. The bag has a spout through which the mortar is squeezed into the joints—it's less messy and will reduce cleanup chores. Clean spilled mortar right away with a wet sponge. Wait until the mortar will hold a thumbprint and then finish the joints with a jointing tool. Cover the surface with plastic or burlap (you'll need to keep it wet) and let it cure for 3 to 4 days. Then install edging if you have not already done so.

After you have swept sand in the joints between the stones, sweep the surface clean and wet it with a fine mist from the hose. Continue adding sand and misting until the joints are full. Don't wash the sand out of the joints.

CONCRETE PATIO

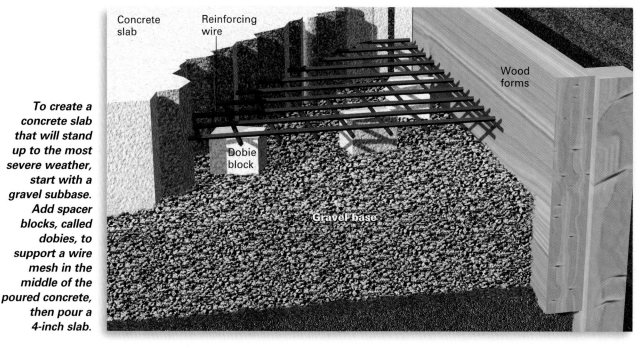

Concrete slab

Reinforcing wire

Wood forms

Dobie block

Gravel base

To create a concrete slab that will stand up to the most severe weather, start with a gravel subbase. Add spacer blocks, called dobies, to support a wire mesh in the middle of the poured concrete, then pour a 4-inch slab.

WORKING WITH CONCRETE

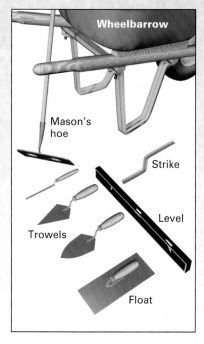

Wheelbarrow

Mason's hoe

Strike

Level

Trowels

Float

Concrete work requires some tools you may not own. Luckily, most are inexpensive to buy or rent. Here's what you need:

■ A carpenter's level to level forms and base material.

■ A garden rake to smooth the gravel base.

■ A clean wheelbarrow and a mason's hoe to mix concrete or mortar by hand. The wheelbarrow should have a steel body and inflatable tire.

■ A long, straight 2×4 (called a strike-off board or screed) to level the surface of poured concrete.

■ A wooden float and a darby to finish the surface smoothly.

■ Various mason's trowels for cutting and smoothing.

■ Edging and jointing tools to create smooth edges and clean control joints.

Other items you'll need for concrete work are a square-edged shovel, clean running water, and plenty of physical endurance. The work is not complicated, but it requires speed, strength, and stamina. Line up at least a few volunteer helpers.

Concrete is one of the most versatile materials for use in patio construction. When wet, it can assume almost any shape, and when cured it will stand up to hard use and extreme weather conditions. It accepts color and texture treatments and costs less than many other building materials.

Poured concrete has its drawbacks, however. Working with it requires strength and stamina; once a pour is started, it must be finished within a couple of hours, depending on weather conditions. (Get helpers, especially for any patio larger than 10×10.) Curing is not immediate—you will have to wait 3 to 7 days before you can use your concrete patio. And after curing, any mistakes made are permanent. The key to successful concrete work is careful preparation.

To estimate quantities, figure the volume of the area (*see page 66*). Figure fifty 80-pound bags of premix for a 100-square-foot, 4-inch slab. That's a little more than a cubic yard of concrete. For larger sites (or if you're not up to mixing), order ready-mix. The supplier will add ingredients to make it workable in most weather conditions.

PREPARING THE SITE

After you have decided where to locate the patio, set temporary stakes at the corners. Make and install batter boards perpendicular to each other about 18 inches beyond the corners, and fasten mason's lines to the center of the crosspieces. Level the lines with a line

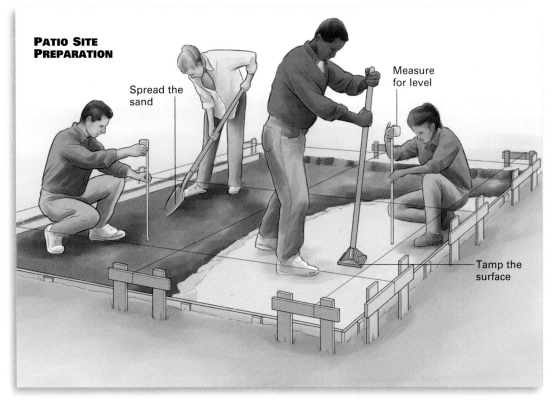

PATIO SITE PREPARATION

Spread the sand

Measure for level

Tamp the surface

To prepare the patio site, measure and mark the perimeter, setting batter boards so lines are square and intersect at the patio corners. Excavate the area and level a sand or gravel base.

level and make sure they're at the same height on the crosspieces.

SQUARE CORNERS: Measure out 3 feet on one of the lines and mark the measurement with tape. On the intersecting line, measure out 4 feet and mark it also. Now measure across, between the tape marks. If they are 5 feet apart, the corners are square. Move the lines on the batter boards until the measurement between the marks is 5 feet.

If you are installing wide edging (timbers, concrete forms, or perpendicular flat brick), attach a second set of lines parallel to the first and separated by the width of the edging. Skip this step for narrow edging, and remember that the mason's lines represent the outside edge of the patio, including the edging. Lower each line in the direction you want slope for drainage (1 inch for every 4 lineal feet).

At each intersection, drop a plumb bob and mark the spot with a stake. Run a tight line between the stakes at ground level and mark it with chalk or spray paint.

EXCAVATING

Start digging along the ground line with a square-edged shovel. Then remove the sod and soil. Dig a ledge at the depth of the edging and then dig a perimeter trench to an 8-inch depth (measure down from the mason's lines to be sure the excavation is consistent). Excavate the remaining area and

install grid lines to make the depth uniformly sloped for drainage (see page 48). Moisten the soil and tamp it with a rented power tamper.

BUILDING FORMS

Poured concrete must be contained by forms—either by permanent edging or temporary forms. You can assemble the forms in the excavated site, but it's easier to do as much of the assembly as possible on the surrounding ground. If the forms will be permanent, use pressure-treated, redwood, or cedar lumber rated for ground contact.

For rectangular temporary forms, use 2×8 stock. Attach 2×4 stakes (with duplex nails) to the corners of each form and at 2-foot intervals. Splice long forms together with ½-inch plywood cleats screwed to the outside of the forms.

To create curved forms, you have three choices:

KERFED WOOD: Make ½-inch cuts (at 1-inch intervals) in 8-inch-high pieces of ¾-inch stock. The board will bend at the kerfs (the cutouts) but will not break on gentle curves.

PLYWOOD: Cut 8-inch strips of ¼-inch plywood.

SHEET METAL: Use 16-gauge (¹⁄₁₆-inch) pieces of sheet metal cut to 8-inch widths.

No matter what material you use, drive stakes along the curve—inside and out— and fasten the forms to the exterior stakes. Remove the interior stakes before pouring.

CONCRETE PATIO
continued

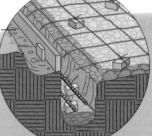

Expansion strip

If your area is subject to ground heave, dig a perimeter footing. In cold climates, extend it beneath the frost line.

Stake or brace forms carefully. Set stakes at least every 4 feet, closer on curves. At joints, nail forms to one stake, or stake and brace as shown.

For small, rounded corners, form the curve with a piece of sheet metal. Backfill soil behind the curve for support.

ESTIMATING CONCRETE

Concrete is measured in cubic yards. To estimate how much you will need, compute the volume of your site in cubic feet (length×width×depth). Divide the result by 27. For example, a slab 4 inches thick and 10 feet square contains 1.2 cubic yards (10×10=100×.33=33÷27=1.2). Add 10 percent to your estimate when ordering dry mix or premix. If you order ready-mix, round up to the nearest quarter cubic yard.

Every cubic yard of concrete requires about 3,200 pounds of dry mix (40 bags at 80 pounds, or just more than 50 bags at 60 pounds).

ORDERING CONCRETE: Bags of premixed dry concrete are the most convenient for small jobs. Mixing your own concrete from separate ingredients is usually the least expensive. For large jobs, buying ready-mixed concrete from a delivery service can save more in time than it costs in money.

If you plan to have the wooden forms become permanent features of your patio, use treated or rot-resistant wood. If possible, buy lumber that is long enough to span the entire excavation so you won't have to butt joints. Cover the top edges of the forms with tape to protect them from concrete stains and set the stakes an inch lower than the top surface. The stakes will be hidden by landscaping later.

■ Make sure the forms follow the correct slope as you install them. Measure down from your grid lines.

■ Align the inside edges of the forms directly under the perimeter string lines.

■ If the forms are temporary, coat the inside edges with a commercial releasing agent so that you can pull them away later, after the concrete has cured.

DIVIDER STRIPS

Divider strips section the surface. They are decorative, help keep the concrete from cracking, and divide the work into more manageable sections.

If your patio will be larger than 8×8, you will need divider strips—or you will need to cut control joints in the surface (*see "Finishing Concrete," page 69*). Install divider strips every 8 feet in each direction, using 2× stock staked at 2-foot intervals. Drive the stakes an inch below the strips so they will be covered by the pour. Divider strips are permanent; tape the top edges. Seal redwood or cedar; pressure-treated wood won't need it.

PREPARING THE BASE

Spread a 4-inch base of gravel—crushed rock or class-5 pea gravel—on a firm soil base. Rake it evenly, then pack it with a power tamper or a plate compactor. A hand tamper is okay for small jobs, but you'll get a workout. Tamp until the surface is smooth, solid, and consistently 4 inches below the anticipated level of the finished slab surface.

For a stronger patio, reinforce the concrete with wire mesh (6×6 10/10). Lay the wire on 2-inch concrete dobies, tying it to the dobies, and overlap the ends by 4 inches. Cut the mesh with a hacksaw or wire cutters. Be cautious, however—the wire can spring back quickly, and it's very sharp.

MIXING CONCRETE

Depending on how much concrete you need, you have three choices for mixing it. In all cases, wear goggles, gloves, and a dust mask. Portland cement can cause severe burns.

SMALL SPOTS:
For small areas, 10 square feet or less, use premix in bags. Prepared dry mixes cost a few cents more per pound than separate ingredients, but are worthwhile for the convenience, especially in small batches. There's no measuring—just add water and mix in a wheelbarrow or mortar box. An area this size will call for about five 80-pound bags.

COMPACT PATIOS: For up to 10×10 feet, mix ingredients in a wheelbarrow or rental power mixer (*see mix recipe, page 66*).
■ To mix concrete in a wheelbarrow, measure (in shovelfuls) the amount of sand, aggregate and portland cement. Mix all the dry ingredients well with a hoe. Form a hollow in the middle and add water. Pull the dry ingredients into the center, working the mixture until it has an even consistency.
■ Power mixers are available in several sizes. A rental shop should be able to recommend one that's right for your project. Set the ingredients near the mixer so you won't have to carry them each time, and block the mixer wheels to keep it from abandoning your job.
■ Before starting, measure out the water; pour about 10 percent of it in the mixer. Start the mixer and add the dry ingredients.
■ Let the mixer run, adding water a little at a time until it reaches the right consistency. Tip the mixer to pour the concrete into a wheelbarrow, and roll it to the site.

Before pouring any mixture of your own, scoop out a small amount with a shovel and test it with a trowel. The concrete should hold its shape when sliced with the edge of the trowel, but should be wet enough that you can smooth it out with the trowel's flat side.

Concrete mixer

Premeasured water

Portland cement

Sand

Gravel

A wheelbarrow and a couple bags of concrete mix will be sufficient for a little job like a stepping stone. For patio areas smaller than 100 square feet, buy the ingredients and rent a power mixer. For larger batches, rely on ready-mix trucks.

BIG PATIOS: Order ready-mix for areas larger than 100 square feet (anything that calls for more than one cubic yard of concrete). Ready-mix requires some additional considerations:
■ Most concrete trucks are too large to drive to the patio site. You may need to pour the mixture from the truck into a wheelbarrow and roll it to the site for pouring. If you can get the truck to the site, make sure it won't damage driveway or lawn surfaces.
■ Some concrete suppliers offer the option of a concrete pump, which delivers the prepared mixture to remote parts of your building site. Any price beats pushing that wheelbarrow.
■ If you live where the ground freezes in the winter, specify air-entrained concrete. It contains microscopic air cells that help prevent cracking.

DRY MIX RECIPE

If you're mixing your own dry mix, here's a handy recipe:
   1 part portland cement
   2 parts sand
   3 parts gravel or aggregate
   ½ part water
Combine the dry ingredients in a mortar box or wheelbarrow and stir in the water, a little at a time. You want a consistency resembling a thick malted milk.

The moisture of the sand you buy and the atmospheric humidity will affect the amount of water you need to add to your concrete. The best way to test it is by feel.

Squeeze a handful of sand, then relax your hand. If it holds together without crumbling, add just ½ part water. If it crumbles or leaves your hand wet, adjust the amount of water as needed.

CONCRETE PATIO
continued

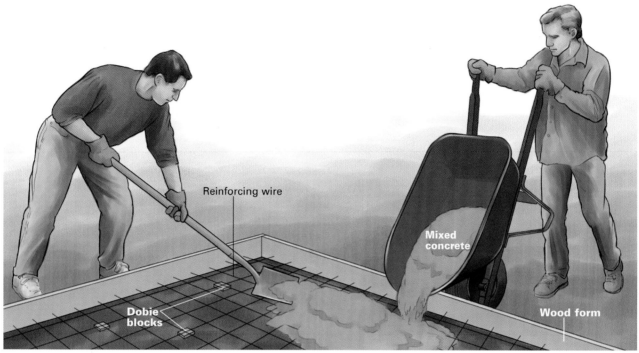

Reinforcing wire

Mixed concrete

Dobie blocks

Wood form

Make sure the concrete is pushed into all the recesses around the forms and the dobies. Voids in the slab will weaken it and lead to cracks in your patio.

POURING CONCRETE

If your project requires so much concrete that you need to order it by the truckload, be sure to have plenty of help available when it arrives. The driver will be able to run the mixer and control the chute, but that's about all. You'll need someone to clear the chute after each load and to roll the wheelbarrow to the site. To keep things moving, have two or three more people at the site to spread the mixture in the forms and finish the surface. More hands (and more wheelbarrows) make the work go faster.

■ Pour the concrete mixture into each form at one corner, and use a flat-edged shovel or a hoe to push it into the edges. Add the next load of concrete as soon as the first one is spread into place, and pour it where the first load ends. Be careful not to work the concrete too hard or to spread it too far; that can make the finished concrete look uneven, and it could weaken it.

■ Once a form is filled, level its surface with a screed board, also called a strikeoff. If the top of the finished concrete will be flush with the forms, use a long, straight 2×4 as a screed board; if the finished surface will be set below the forms, cut out the ends of the screed until it fits inside the forms at the level of the finished surface.

■ With one person at each end of the screed board, slide it gently from side to side in a sawing motion as you pull it across the surface of the concrete. Fill in any low spots by adding fresh concrete, and screed them smooth.

Float the surface—as soon as it's leveled—to remove the major imperfections. Most small floats are made of wood with a wooden handle; larger floats (bull floats) have long handles. Wooden floats are fine, but magnesium floats are smoother and easier to work with. Use a float that's big enough to cover the freshly poured concrete in the fewest passes.

■ Smaller areas can be smoothed with a hand-held float called a darby. Hold the darby flat as you move it across the surface, first in wide arcs. Then tilt it slightly and work in straight pulls.

More people make concrete work easier. For example, one person can mix concrete while another pours it and a third uses a screed board to level it—or two people can work a larger screed board while a third person shovels in any low spots.

■ For large areas, you will need to use a bull float—a smooth board or plate attached with a swivel joint to a long, broom-like handle. Tip the leading edge up slightly as you push the bull float forward, and leave it flat as you bring it gently back.

■ As soon as you have floated the surface, run a trowel along the inside edge of the forms, then let it set up. Now is the time to apply custom finishes (*see page 70*). If you're not custom finishing, wait until the concrete sets up before you start the next steps.

Set-up can take only minutes in hot, dry weather or an hour or more in cool, damp conditions. When the watery sheen is gone, it's ready to finish. Step on it to make sure— your foot should leave no deeper than a ¼-inch impression. Use plywood platforms to support your weight when carrying out the finishing steps.

FINISHING CONCRETE

ROUNDING IT OFF: Rounded edges on a slab not only look nice, they are safer and less subject to chipping. Rounding adds a professional-looking touch to a patio project, and it isn't hard to accomplish.

To give the concrete a rounded edge, slide a trowel between the inside face of the form and the poured concrete. Slide the curved side of the edger in along the form, tipping up its leading edges slightly as you move it forward and back. The edger's curved lip creates a consistent rounded edge on the concrete.

KEEPING IT IN ONE PIECE: No concrete installation can ever be made crack free, but the reinforcing wire mesh will keep your slab together. If you haven't installed expansion strips, give your concrete a place to crack during changes in the weather by cutting control joints in its surface. Because the control joints are cut into the surface of the slab, any cracks will be below the surface. Using a straight board to guide you, cut a control joint in the surface—from end to end—every 8 feet in both directions on a 4-inch slab. You can skip this step if you have installed dividers.

HAND FLOATING: Hand floating gives the surface its final smoothing and prepares it for the finish. Use a wood float for a rough finish or a steel trowel for a smooth finish. A troweled surface will be too slick for a patio, but troweling needs to be done before you apply a broom finish.

THE RIGHT TOOL FOR THE JOB

Several kinds of trowels and floats can help you get an expert finish on your concrete. Each has a distinct purpose.

DARBY
For smoothing reachable areas of concrete; leaves a semi-rough surface.

BULL FLOAT
A long-handled float for smoothing large areas of freshly poured concrete. Useful for surfaces you can't reach across.

HAND FLOAT
For smoothing small areas and for matching patches to the surrounding area.

MAGNESIUM FLOAT
For creating very smooth surfaces. Can produce surfaces that are too slick for walking when wet.

JOINTER
For creating control joints that relieve stress in slabs larger than 8 feet square.

MASON'S TROWEL
A multipurpose tool used for mortaring, shown here creating a smooth edge along a concrete form.

CONCRETE PATIO
continued

WASHED AGGREGATE

Press aggregate into fresh and leveled concrete with a float—just until you can see the tops of the stones. Then sweep the excess and spray until the top half of the stones show.

PAINTING WITH CONCRETE PAINT

Painting concrete is the fastest way to add color to a slab— but the least permanent. The paint wears quickly with use.

USING A SURFACE DYE

TOOLING

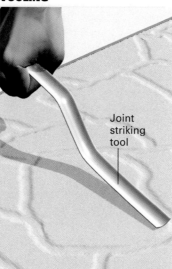

Joint striking tool

FINISH OPTIONS

You can give your patio a distinctive appearance by smooth troweling or broom sweeping. To add more texture or color to concrete slab before it cures, consider these techniques:

EXPOSED AGGREGATE: Divide the project into sections. Pour the concrete to within ½ inch of the forms (you'll be adding aggregate, which will raise the level of the surface). Then float and finish. Sprinkle aggregate across the surface, covering it evenly. Press the aggregate into the wet concrete with a float, long 2×6s, or shovels.

Embed the stones until you can just see the tops. When the surface has hardened enough to support your weight on boards, sweep away the excess around the stones with a stiff brush. Spray it with water until about half of the stone diameter shows.

STAMPING: To press patterns (resembling brick, flagstone, cobblestone, or geometric designs) in fresh concrete, use a stamping form, available from many building supply stores and rental outlets.

If you use stamping forms, rent two or more. You will be able to position the forms more accurately for consistent results.

Set both stamps in place; stand on one, then step onto the other. Impressions should be about an inch deep. Use a joint-striking tool to smooth out the stamped edges.

COLORING: Dyes can be added to the concrete mix before you pour it, in either a one-course or two-course method. The latter involves pouring a 1-inch layer of colored concrete over a partially set slab.

You can get satisfactory results from dyes added after the surface is poured. Dyes on the surface of wet concrete will make a slab look like granite, slate, or sandstone.

Sprinkle about two thirds of the powder on the surface evenly over the slab. When the powder absorbs some of the moisture from the surface, hand float it into the surface and sprinkle the rest of the powder. Let it be absorbed and then float again.

Painting concrete is another coloring option, but is the least desirable because the painted surface will ultimately wear away. If you're going to paint, wait until the concrete has cured for at least 28 days.

TOOLING: After floating, use a joint strike tool to make lines in the wet concrete surface. With practice, you can make free-form shapes that resemble stones. It's easier if you work from a pattern you have drawn earlier. The lines won't erase. If you have a steady

STAMPING

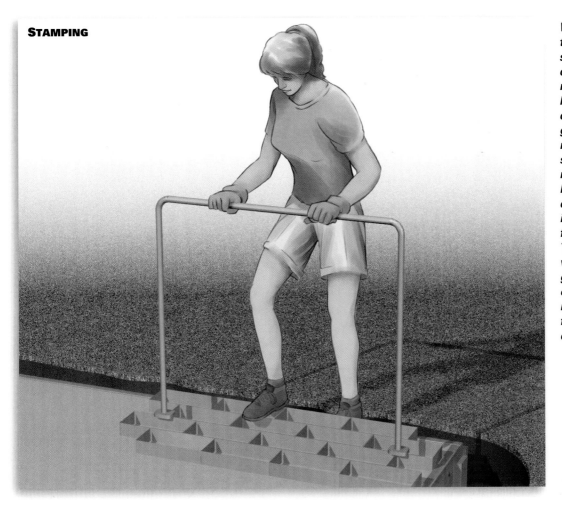

With color treatments and stamping dies, concrete can be made to look like brick pavers, ceramic tile, granite, or even marble. Concrete suppliers and rental shops have forms you can rent to make impressions in fresh concrete. The patterns vary from geometric to ones that resemble flagstone and cobblestone.

hand, you can impress your own patterns into freshly poured concrete. Practice—you only get one chance.

CURING THE SLAB

Concrete needs plenty of time to harden properly. If the moisture content of a concrete slab evaporates too quickly, the surface may become grainy and the entire slab may never reach its potential strength (concrete strength increases as it cures).

The hardening process—called curing—takes at least three days for most patios. For larger projects, in cooler weather, or just to get the best results possible, give the surface a week to cure. During this curing time, there are three ways to keep your slab from drying out prematurely:

DAMPEN: As you'd expect, the best method takes the most time and trouble. Spread blankets over the slab and sprinkle them periodically to keep them damp. After the concrete is firm enough to resist pitting, you can sprinkle it directly with a periodic, gentle spritzing from your garden hose. Remember, the goal is not to drown the new concrete, just to keep its surface damp.

COVER: If you don't have the time or a water source for sprinkling, you need to retard the evaporation of water from your concrete. The simplest solution is to cover the new slab with plastic sheeting. If the temperature is cool, use black plastic because it absorbs more of the warmth of the sunlight. To keep the sheet in place, use stones or lumber scraps to hold down the edges of the plastic around the outside of the concrete forms.

TREAT: You can buy a chemical curing agent to spray or roll onto the slab. Clear or tinted white, these products keep the concrete moist. However, don't use a curing agent if you plan to cover your patio with tile, bricks, or stone. Mortar and tile adhesives will not stick to the treated concrete surface.

Regardless of your concrete-curing method, do not permit new concrete to freeze. If a cold snap during the curing process threatens to dip below freezing, cover the concrete with straw or blankets.

TILE PATIO

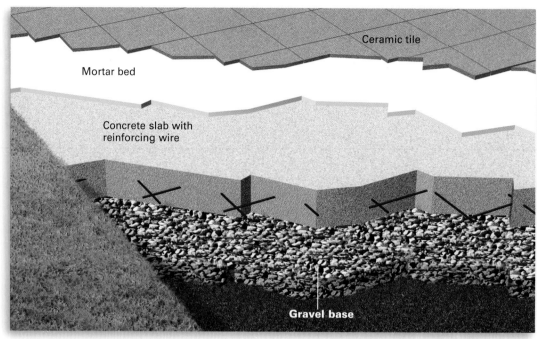

Tile and grout are inflexible materials, so they are vulnerable to movement caused by temperature changes. To prevent tile and grout from cracking, reinforce its concrete slab with wire mesh, and place control joints at 8-foot intervals in the concrete.

Ceramic tile

Mortar bed

Concrete slab with reinforcing wire

Gravel base

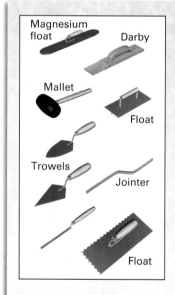

Magnesium float

Darby

Mallet

Float

Trowels

Jointer

Float

WORKING WITH TILE

If you haven't installed tile before, you probably don't have all the tools you need for a tile patio. Don't compromise; get the right tools before starting your project. Most tools for working with tile are inexpensive, and are easier to buy than to rent. One exception is a specialty cutter, such as a wet tile saw, which you can rent from a tile supplier or a rental shop. Here's what you'll need:

■ To spread the mortar evenly, use a square-notched trowel.

■ For setting the tiles firmly in the mortar, use a rubber mallet; a heavy mallet with a large face is easier to use safely on large tiles.

■ To cut tiles, use a circular saw with a masonry blade, a hand-operated tile cutter, a wet tile saw, or a pair of nippers, depending which one is best for the task. Ask your supplier for advice.

■ For filling the spaces between tiles after the mortar has set, use a grout float designed for the type of grout you buy.

■ To wipe away excess mortar or grout before it dries, use a large clean sponge and clean water.

Each project has different requirements, which vary with the kind of tile and the local climate. Ask your supplier for tips about your region, about the tiles that match the variations of your climate, and whether you need special materials, such as plastic spacers or backing strips for caulk.

Tile can transform any spot in your landscape into the most pleasant area on your property. Depending on your choice of material, tile can look rugged or refined, and will last for years if it is installed properly on a stable foundation. The single most important task in preparing to build a tile patio is a level and flat concrete slab.

PREPARING AN OLD SLAB

If you already have a concrete slab, it may be suitable for use as a tile base. Check it thoroughly. Dig down to see if the slab is at least 4 inches thick and rests on a 4-inch gravel base. If you have a level 3-inch slab on a 4-inch gravel bed, you can add concrete.

Look for cracks, severe chipping or sunken spots. If these are present, pull the old slab out and lay a new one.

Lay a 2×4 across its surface. Tile needs a surface with no more than $\frac{1}{8}$ inch variance in every 10 feet. Knock out high spots and minor flaking with a sledge and fill them and low spots with patching concrete (*see "Caring for an Older Patio," page 90*).

If the slab is intact and level, simply clean it with a solution of muriatic acid (1 part acid to 4 parts water). Then rinse it well and let it dry before applying the mortar.

Whether you use an existing concrete slab or pour a new one, make sure it meets building code requirements for your area.

NEW SLAB PREPARATION

Before laying out your patio, figure its dimensions so that you have an even number of tiles, or so that you know the pattern will fit with minimum cutting. Divide the tile (or pattern) dimensions into the patio length and width and adjust if necessary. Then lay out the patio area with batter boards and mason's lines (*see pages 44-46 for more information*).

Level the lines; then slope them slightly for drainage (1 inch for every 4 feet). Add lines for wide edging and level and slope them also. Square the corners by measuring out a 3-4-5 triangle on the lines and drop a plumb bob to mark the corners. Tie lines at ground level between the corner stakes and mark them with chalk or spray paint (*see page 45*).

Excavate the patio area to a depth that will accommodate the 4-inch gravel base, the 4-inch concrete slab, and the thickness of the mortar and materials. Subtract an inch or so from this depth to raise your patio slightly above ground. Tie grid lines to help keep the excavation sloped correctly throughout. Install forms (make them from 2× stock) attached to stakes driven in the ground. Next, pour in the gravel bed and screed it, using the forms as guides. Tamp the gravel to a depth of 4 inches. Now you're ready for the pour.

POURING THE SLAB

For sites under 10 square feet, mix premixed concrete. It comes in bags; all you have to do is add water. For sites up to 100 square feet, mix the dry ingredients or order ready-mix. Ready-mix is a must for larger patios.

Pour the concrete level with the forms, work a shovel in it to remove air pockets, and use a long 2×4 to screed it level with the forms. Finish the concrete with a wooden float but do not smooth it with a metal trowel—a slightly rough surface gives the mortar a tooth to bind it to the slab. Then let the concrete set up. Do not round the edges with an edging tool, but when the concrete is set, run control joints with a jointer—every 8 feet in both directions. They give the concrete a place to crack under the surface and keep the tile from cracking. (Add control joints to an existing slab by cutting shallow grooves in it with a circular saw and a masonry blade.) Then let the concrete cure (keep it moist with plastic) for 3 to 7 days. Once it has cured, remove the forms and scrub it down with water and a broom.

TESTING THE LAYOUT

Without using any mortar, set tiles in place across the slab to see how they look. You don't need to lay out the entire patio, just set enough tiles to get an idea how the finished surface will appear on all sides.

Mark the center of the patio by using lines from each of the corners, and start the dry layout at the center point, extending the tiles to all sides of the foundation. If one side ends with a full tile and the opposite side has only part of a tile, move the center point so both sides will have tiles of the same size (cut or uncut). Mark the locations of the control joints—you'll need to know where they are when you're setting the tile. When the layout is accurate, draw reference lines that show where you will need to begin spreading the mortar.

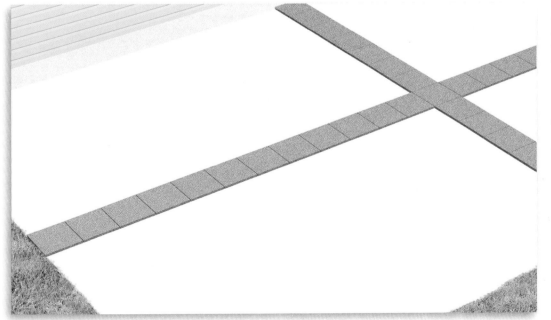

Before you apply mortar, set a full row of tiles in both directions to see where you might need to cut and place partial tiles. If the patio is not a square or a rectangle, place test tiles in all directions before you apply the mortar.

TILE PATIO
continued

Spread mortar evenly across a surface with a notched trowel. The teeth of the trowel should not quite touch the concrete surface below.

APPLYING MORTAR

Ideally you should apply the mortar when the outside temperature is between 60° and 70° F. Don't work in direct sunlight—the mortar will set too quickly.

Mix latex thin-set mortar in a 5-gallon bucket, following the manufacturer's directions. Mortar mixes much easier if you use a ½-inch drill with a mixing blade (most of them look like a miniature fan on a long shaft). Let the mortar set for about 10 minutes, then mix it again. Start at the center of the patio surface and spread a thin coat of mortar with the flat side of a ¼×¼ notched trowel. Then rake the spread mortar at a 45-degree angle with the notched side of the trowel; don't scrape through to the slab, however. The grooves created by the notches give the mortar a place to expand and level under the bottom of the tile when you push it in place. Start with enough to lay just one or two tiles at first. As you get accustomed to the material, you'll develop a rhythm and gain some confidence. Then work in sections you can complete in 10 minutes.

CUTTING TILES

You can have tiles cut by your supplier, but with the right tools, tile is not difficult to cut yourself. And you can rent the tools you need from your tile dealer or from most general rental centers. Here are some options:
■ A power tile saw can save you hours of effort and piles of wasted material if your pattern calls for more than a few cuts.
■ If you expect to cut only a few tiles, rent a manual snap cutter. It's easy to use and the results will have you feeling like a real craftsman.
■ You also can cut tile with a masonry blade attached to your circular saw. Always be sure the tile is clamped firmly in place.
■ If you do your own cutting, be sure to wear protection for your eyes, ears, and hands.
■ For cutting unusual angles or contours, score the tile with a glass cutter and snap away small pieces with a pair of tile nippers.

Troweled
mortar

Plastic
spacers

Many tiles have ridges on the sides, called lugs, that keep them far enough apart to allow grout to fill the joints. If the tiles you choose don't have lugs, or if you want them spaced farther apart than the lugs, use X-shape plastic spacers.

SETTING TILES

Set as many full tiles as possible, using spacers to keep them spaced for grouting. Drop each tile in place with a slight twist and tap it with a rubber mallet (or make a beater block from a short length of 2×4 covered with scrap carpet.) Set the beater block on the tile, carpet side down, and tap with a hammer. The block not only sets the tile, but also levels adjacent units.

The mortar should begin to squeeze up between the tiles as you press the next one down, but if it comes up more than half the thickness of the tiles, you're using too much. You need to leave enough room for grout and for caulk backing strips at the joints.

Every now and then, pick up a set tile to make sure the mortar adheres evenly across its back. Use mason's lines across the surface to help you keep the rows straight and check each section for level with a straightedge.

As you work, remove the spacers from tiles that have had a few minutes to set up. It's much more difficult to remove the spacers after the mortar has hardened completely.

Continue spreading mortar in both directions away from the intersection of the layout lines, taking care to leave yourself room to work. As you get closer to each edge, have the partial tiles ready so you can set them in place without searching for them or having to cut new ones.

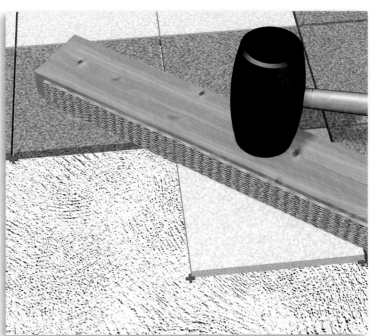

To set a tile in mortar without disturbing the tiles around it, cover a piece of lumber with carpet, lay it over the tile, and tap it with a rubber mallet.

Once you have set all the tiles, remove remaining spacers and check gaps between the tiles. With the tip of a masonry trowel, gently scrape out excess mortar. Press backing strips into the joints at the locations of the control joints in the slab (*marked as shown on page 73*). Let the mortar set for at least a day before adding the grout.

TILE PATIO
continued

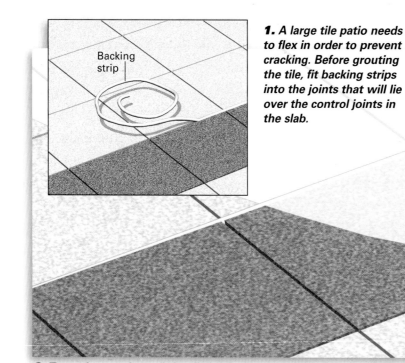

Backing strip

1. *A large tile patio needs to flex in order to prevent cracking. Before grouting the tile, fit backing strips into the joints that will lie over the control joints in the slab.*

2. *To push grout into all the tile joints evenly, sweep the grout float across the tiles at a 45-degree angle. The broad side of the grout float should move in a diagonal over the corners of the tiles. If the float is parallel or perpendicular to the tiles, it will pull grout from the joints instead of working it in. Clean up grout haze quickly, or it will be very difficult to remove.*

3. *Remove the backing strips, and fill the control joints with siliconized caulk that matches the grout.*

APPLYING GROUT

When the mortar is completely dry, prepare grout recommended for your tile. Follow the manufacturer's directions for mixing the grout, and keep it in a container you can seal. Grout used for exterior applications should contain latex, which is easy to clean up and needs little time to cure. If yours does not, ask your dealer if you can add latex.

With a mason's trowel, scoop grout from the mixing container and place it on the tiles. Hold a grout float at a 45-degree angle, push the float into the grout, and spread grout across the tiles with the trailing edge of the float.

Move the float at angles to the tile pattern so that the grout will fill and not pull out of the joints. Spread grout in alternating directions with the float to force out any air trapped in the joints. When all the joints are full, clean off the grout float and use it to scrape excess grout from the tile surface. Be careful not to press the float into the joints.

CLEANING UP

Check the manufacturer's directions for drying time before cleaning. This may be 15 minutes to an hour, or even more. But if you wait too long, the cleanup will be much harder—cured grout is almost impossible to remove. Check the grout with the point of the mason's trowel to be sure it has hardened.

To remove grout haze, wipe the tile surface with a rough-textured, dry sponge and a clean, dry cloth.

Remove the caulk backing strips from the joints over the control joints in the slab, and fill the empty joints with caulk that matches the grout.

Apply grout sealer to the finished joints, taking care not to get sealer on the tiles themselves. You may have to wait several days for the grout to fully cure before you apply sealer—ask your dealer for the waiting period appropriate to your sealer. Wipe away any extra sealer, and buff the tile again after the sealer dries.

LAYING ADOBE TILE

Adobe blocks are sun dried and soft, and they may vary a bit in shape from one to the next. That's part of their charm, but it makes for a little extra work when laying them. Without lugs, you need to space the blocks by hand. Push down and turn each one as you set it. Add dirt fill or sand as soon as you can, and gently tamp the fill with a board. Use the tamping board gently to avoid moving the blocks.

Adobe blocks look comfortable and familiar, and they give your patio a casual air. Long associated with the Southwest, adobe block is gaining popularity as a paving material in other regions as well. That's because some manufacturers now add stabilizers, such as asphalt, that make the blocks more durable and less porous. Adobe still has geographic limits. If you live in a climate where winter temperatures freeze, they will crack when the moisture they absorb swells as it freezes. Check with your supplier to see if they are suitable for your patio.

Traditional adobe (without asphalt) absorbs water easily and then breaks when it freezes, so it's also poorly suited for use in northern climates.

■ Because adobe blocks are fragile, the foundation that supports them should be perfectly flat. Excavate the patio site to the thickness of the adobe blocks, plus a sand bed and gravel subbase deep enough to hold the blocks at ground level.

■ Adobe works with or without edging materials. If you want to contain the patio visually, use a border that complements the adobe. Pressure-treated landscape timbers are popular as edging for adobe because they share its rough and heavy look. Other options include loose fill, plantings, or adobe blocks of different sizes.

■ After concrete, adobe is the heaviest patio material most homeowners would want to handle. To prevent strain or injury while working with large pavers, have an assistant help you lift, place, and adjust the blocks.

■ Place blocks in a pattern that complements your property. If necessary, you can cut adobe blocks easily.

■ Once you have all the adobe blocks in place, fill in the joints with sand or mortar for easy maintenance, Tamp sand with the end of a board. You can even fill the joints with soil and plant them with light ground cover to give the entire patio an organic look. Use a piece of scrap lumber to tamp down the filler.

PAVER PATIO

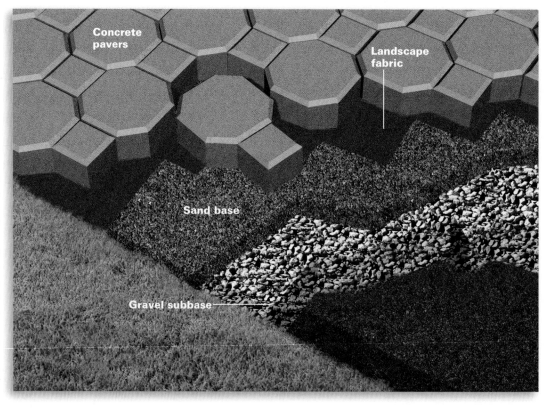

Concrete pavers are available in several designs and colors. One of the most popular combines squares and octagons for a pattern of alternating shapes. The pavers are cast with lugs on the sides to create a small gap between each pair of adjoining blocks.

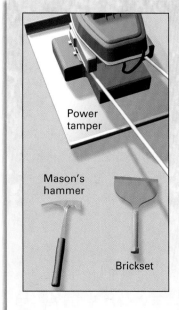

Power tamper

Mason's hammer

Brickset

WORKING WITH CONCRETE PAVERS

You shouldn't need many specialized tools to lay concrete pavers, and the ones you do need are relatively inexpensive. Items you need to buy include a masonry blade for cutting pavers with a circular saw, a mason's hammer (if you don't already have one), and a brickset.

The only item you'll need to rent is a power tamper for compacting the subbase and for packing sand in the joints of the finished surface. A hand tamper will do for some small areas, but a power tamper will usually do a better and faster job.

■ For setting pavers without damaging them, use a rubber mallet.
■ To cut individual pavers to special sizes or shapes, use a circular saw with a masonry blade. Always wear eye protection when cutting concrete pavers.
■ If you have more than a few pavers to cut, have your supplier do it.

oncrete pavers combine the design versatility of tile with the easy installation of brick. They are made of cast concrete in sizes and patterns to fit any style or space and are designed to be set in a sand bed over a gravel base.

PLANNING THE LAYOUT

To make accurate estimates of how much material you will need, draw a trial layout on graph paper with ¼-inch increments.

Start with the outline of an approximate patio size and draw it to scale of ¼ inch = 1 inch. Then draw in your pattern to scale. Most patterns will lend themselves to sectioning—figure how much area one section covers and the number of sections of the same size your patio dimensions will accommodate.

Adjust the final patio size so your patterns will be complete with a minimum of cutting. Then count the number of pavers in each section and multiply by the number of even sections to estimate material quantities.

Most suppliers will allow you to return unused materials, so buy 10 to 15 percent more than you expect to need. A leisurely return trip is more pleasant than interrupting your work because you ran out of materials.

LAYING OUT THE SITE

Using the same methods discussed on pages 44-46 for a sand-based brick patio, lay out the site with batter boards and mason's lines. Square the corners, set corner stakes, and mark ground lines. Be sure to slope your mason's lines by 1 inch every 4 feet to achieve proper drainage.

EXCAVATION

Excavate the site to a uniformly sloped depth of 6 inches (4 inches for gravel and 2 inches for sand bedding) plus the thickness of the pavers. Measure the excavation depth from the sloped mason's and grid lines. Moisten the soil and tamp it with a power tamper.

EDGING

Precast concrete paver designs include individual units made for edging. Use them by themselves or combine them with other edging materials.

■ To create a visible border, such as pressure-treated landscape timbers, place the edging materials in a trench on the outside of the patio area. Dig the trench to the depth of the edging material plus several inches for a gravel base for drainage. Bricks used as a border would be similarly set, but in a concrete bed for stability.

■ To make a hidden border that holds the pavers in place, set rigid plastic edging along the inside of the patio area. Hold the edging in place with metal spikes. The top ridge of the edging should extend above the sand base by ½ to ¾ of the paver thickness. Backfill behind the edging with tamped soil and cover the top with soil so that it can't be seen.

POURING THE SUBBASE

■ When the excavation and edging is complete, drive several small stakes inside the site. Set the top of each stake at 4 inches above the excavation surface.

■ Pour gravel into the site—level with the stakes—and spread it evenly with a garden rake. Check the surface with a long, flat 2×4 to make sure it is uniform. Measure the surface from the mason's lines to make sure it's sloped correctly, or use a screed with cutouts riding on the edging surface.

When the subbase is level and consistent, compact the gravel with a tamper. Add landscaping fabric to prevent weeds from growing through.

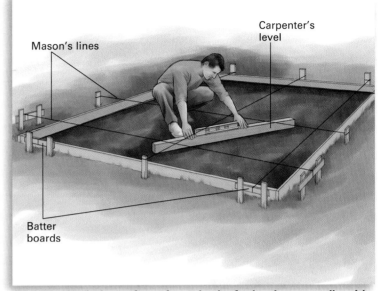

Mason's lines

Carpenter's level

Batter boards

You can check the surface of a patio site for level most easily with a carpenter's level set on a long, straight 2×4. Remember to slope for drainage.

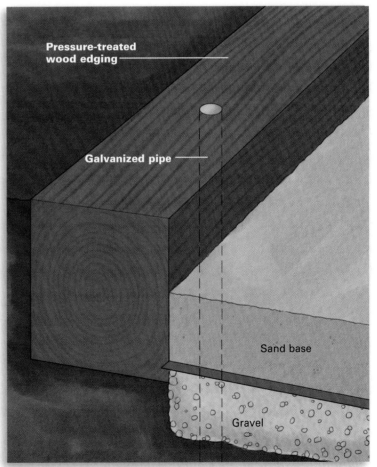

Pressure-treated wood edging

Galvanized pipe

Sand base

Gravel

Without an edge to hold them in place, concrete pavers can shift and break up the pattern you created. A border made of pressure-treated wood, whether smooth posts or rough landscape timbers, visually defines the patio and keeps the pavers in line.

PAVER PATIO
continued

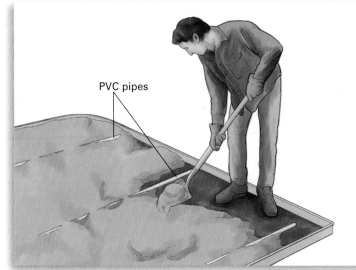

To create an even surface with a loose material like sand, lay PVC pipes on the surface before pouring in the sand. Add sand until it covers the pipes.

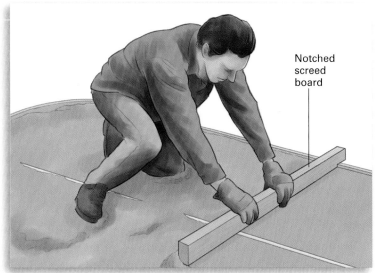

Draw a screed board across the PVC pipes to level the surface. Because the sand bed will probably be lower than any edging materials, notch one end of the screed board accordingly.

Concrete is especially hard, so use a specialty tool designed for the purpose if you need to cut any pavers. You can get a tub saw from most rental shops, tile stores, or from some concrete contractors.

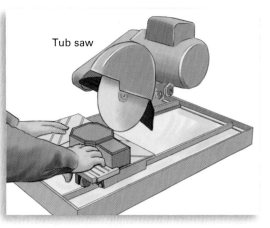

CREATING THE BASE

■ Shovel washed sand into the patio site and spread it with a garden rake. Push the sand gently into the edges and corners, taking care not to disrupt the landscaping fabric or subbase.
■ Check the bedding for slope and consistency, and adjust the surface as needed. Mark a piece of pipe at 2 inches and push it in the sand or lay lengths of 2-inch PVC pipe about every 3 to 4 feet. Make a screed with cutouts that will ride on the edging at the thickness of your pavers (or directly on top of the PVC pipe). Screed the sand, working the board back and forth across the surface.
■ Soak the sand base, using a garden hose with a sprayer attachment set to fine mist. Compact the wet sand with a power tamper.
■ Fill low spots and indentations with added sand, and tamp flat again.
■ Continue adding sand and tamping until the base is consistent across the entire site. Pull out the PVC pipe, if you've used them, fill in the recesses left by the pipe and tamp again.

CUTTING PAVERS

Although you can reduce the amount of cut pavers by making your design come out in even sizes, cutting a paver is probably unavoidable. Concrete paver is hard—as hard as tile and almost as thick as brick, so they're difficult to cut. You can break pavers with a hand sledge and a bricklayer's chisel, but you're not likely to get clean edges. To make your cuts clean, rent a tile saw that handles concrete, or use a masonry blade on a circular saw (be sure to clamp the paver tightly and wear safety goggles).

SETTING THE PAVERS

■ Starting in a corner, lay the first few pavers in place. If you are using rigid plastic edging, the pavers should fit snugly against it. For other edging, leave a space for sand. With a rubber mallet, tap each paver on the top to set it in the sand base, and on the side to make sure it fits well against the next paver.
■ Most pavers are cast with spacing lugs; push the pavers tightly against each other. If your pavers don't have lugs, use 1/8-inch plywood to space them.
■ As you lay more pavers, work in two directions to keep your design from shifting to either side. To check your progress, look at

No matter how carefully you prepare the sand bed, some pavers will need a little help before they line up just right. If a paver rides a bit too high, tap it with a rubber mallet. If that isn't enough, take the paver out and remove a small amount of sand before replacing it. You also may need to add sand to fill low spots.

Doing It All Yourself

Casting your own pavers takes time, but you can create exactly the look you want. Make forms of 1×4 lumber with plywood bottoms to cast loose pavers, or dig shallow recesses in the ground to cast them in place.

Experiment with different colors, shapes, and textures. To fit the average person's walking stride, set the finished pavers with the centers about 18 inches apart.

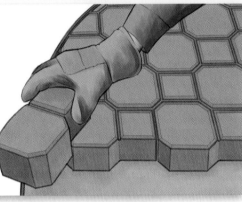

Place cut pavers in the same order as the main pattern. If you wait until all the uncut pavers are in place, you may have trouble getting the others to fit.

the pattern after setting every few pavers, and test the surface with a carpenter's level or a straight 2×4.

■ If the surface has low spots (and it's almost impossible to avoid them), remove a few pavers, add sand, and replace the pavers. High spots can sometimes be fixed with a few more taps from the mallet. Make adjustments as you work; you won't want to start over.

■ After you pave every few square feet, stretch a mason's line across the surface to make sure the layout is straight.

■ After you pave more than half of the patio in any direction, and before you reach the opposite side, measure the remaining distance. Then measure the paved section to see how the remaining pavers will fit. If the distance can't be filled with whole pavers, you may prefer to move the edging on the far side instead of cutting an entire course of pavers.

FINISHING THE JOINTS

■ Cover all the pavers with washed sand and spread it with a push broom. Sweep from all directions to pack sand well into the joints.
■ When the joints are full, sweep the remaining sand from the patio, being careful not to sweep it out of the joints. Wet the surface with water and tamp it with a power tamper. Let it dry, and check the joints to make sure they are all filled. Add sand to any joints that need more, sweep the area clean, and soak it again.

Once you have all the pavers in place, spread a layer of clean, dry sand over the surface. Get washed sand from a building supply store; it's often sold as "play sand" for children's sandboxes. Sweep sand into the joints from several directions, collect the excess, and wet the surface with a garden hose. Continue adding sand and spraying until the joints are full.

WALKWAYS AND STAIRS

TREADS AND RISERS

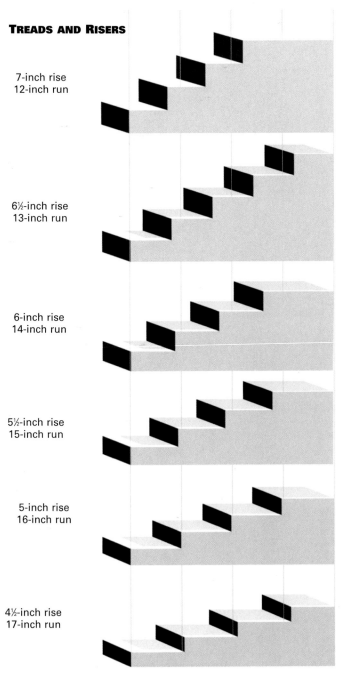

7-inch rise
12-inch run

6½-inch rise
13-inch run

6-inch rise
14-inch run

5½-inch rise
15-inch run

5-inch rise
16-inch run

4½-inch rise
17-inch run

RISE AND RUN

Measure the rise (height) and run (length) of the stair location before laying stairs out. To calculate the number of steps you will need, divide the total rise by the step height you want, rounding fractions up. For example, if the slope is 48 inches high and you plan 7-inch risers, you will have seven of them.

For evenly spaced treads, divide the run by the number of risers you've calculated. For example, each of seven treads on an 84-inch run would be 12 inches deep.

Walkways and stairs let you connect different parts of your property with one another. A simple flight of steps can expand the useful area of your patio, and a paved path can establish or reinforce a design theme.

BUILDING WALKWAYS

PLANNING: Walking paths are essentially the same thing as patios—just narrower. The same design and construction techniques apply to walkways as to patios, with a few additional tips:

■ Choose materials that match or complement the patio. To use a walkway as a visual transition, coordinate the materials with the areas at both ends of the walk.

■ Set obvious borders along the edges of a walkway—edgings define the walk and contain materials.

■ Make walkways wide enough for people with limited mobility, who may need to use walkers or wheelchairs. This makes the patio accessible to all your guests, and more comfortable as well.

■ For comfort and safety, a walkway should be consistent and smooth. Even if it's set on level ground, it should slope slightly for drainage. Pathway slope can be less than patio slope (¾ of an inch every 4 lineal feet).

■ On a gentle rise over a long distance, you may prefer to build a walkway instead of many shallow steps. If your building site has a severe slope, or if you need to add a retaining wall to add stairs, ask a landscape architect to review your plans.

BUILDING STAIRS

DESIGN: A stairway can be a functional and decorative extension of your patio. Stairways can help you include more of your property in a coordinated design. A paved or poured stairway generally looks informal compared to one built of lumber, but the dimensions are just as important for safety and comfort.

MATERIALS: Use the same materials and installation methods for steps as you would for your patio surface.

RISE AND RUN: No matter what materials you use, make sure the steps are the same height and depth from one to the next. The illustration (*see left*) shows the most common combinations of rise and run, as well as the formula for calculating rise and run for your own stairway.

CREATING THE LAYOUT: Choose the materials you want to use, where you want to place the stairway, and how long and wide it should be. Then start measuring.

■ With 2×4 stakes, mark the points at

Unless you have worked with concrete before, you may want to get the help of a professional before pouring concrete stairs. The forms must allow the concrete to flow from one step to the next, and the steps have to be poured in sequence from the bottom to the top. Do this job yourself only if you're experienced.

the top and bottom of the slope. Use a water level between the two stakes to find the total rise. Find the distance from the top of the slope to the level mark on the lower stake with a tape measure. This is the total run.

■ Using the formula (*see "Rise and Run," opposite page*), figure out the number of steps you need to make. If your slope is too steep for the combinations shown, try setting the stairway at an angle or use a landing and change directions. Don't make the steps too steep.

EXCAVATING THE SLOPE: Remove the sod from the slope with a square-edged shovel.

■ Cut straight down where each riser will go; the measurements don't need to be exact yet. If you pour concrete for the steps or as a base for other materials, the forms will determine the final height of each step.

BUILDING THE FORMS: Cut forms for each step from 2×4 or 2×6 lumber, and set the forms in place. Secure the forms with stakes.

■ Pack the soil well with a hand tamper, and pour a layer of gravel in each form. Add dobie blocks and reinforcing wire mesh for larger steps or in regions with severe winters.

POURING CONCRETE: Mix concrete and pour it in the forms, using the same methods as for a patio (*see page 68*).

■ Level the surface with a screed board, and smooth it with a hand-held float. If you like, brush the surface to increase traction.

■ Let the concrete cure for the recommended time, usually 3 days to a week. If the design includes bricks or pavers, set them in mortar on the concrete when it has cured.

FINISHING THE STAIRWAY: When the stairway structure is complete, add edging or decorative elements. To soften the look and feel of a concrete stairway, add railroad ties at the edge of each step, level with the surface.

IT ONLY LOOKS EASY

A well-built flagstone stairway, one that is comfortable to use, is a pleasure to see. But building one takes a tremendous amount of effort and patience. First, you have to make sure the flagstones are smooth and flat enough to use as steps. Second, you need to grade the slope for the stairway to create a rise and run that will match most people's strides. Third, and hardest of all, you have to set the flagstones securely in the ground. Just getting the stones in place isn't enough. They need to be level so that no one will trip on them, close enough together that people can step easily from one to the next, and set at even intervals of height. If you choose to create a flagstone stairway, be prepared to spend plenty of time adjusting the individual steps. Then get ready to hear others comment about how natural it looks.

DECORATIVE STONE WALLS

DRY-STACKED STONE

If you need to build a wall in a hurry, don't choose dry-stacked stone. Just like a flagstone patio, a dry-stacked stone wall requires extensive fitting and refitting. To get it right, be prepared to take plenty of time.

Stone is simple and organic, and it adds a sense of natural permanence to any patio. Stone retaining walls hold back the earth and help create level ground from slopes. You can build a mortared stone wall or one that is dry set—the stones are held together by gravity and friction. Mortared walls will require a footing. Dry-set stone do not need a footing, but do require a gravel bed for support and drainage.

STONE SHOPPING

Take the measurements and the design ideas for your wall to a landscape specialist or garden center. Professional advice can help take the guesswork out of stone selection and materials estimates. Remember that rounded boulders are more difficult to set. Flat stone is much easier to stack and fit. After the stone is delivered, sort it near the site; pile it by size and shape. Use a wheelbarrow to move the stone along the sides of the wall site. Set aside the longest stones for bonding stones—you'll set them at right angles to bind the wall from front to back.

DRY-FIT

Dry walls should be stacked two-thirds as thick as they are high, and no taller than 3 feet. A dry wall will rise and resettle with changes in the ground temperature, so it won't require a footing. Dig out a trench a foot deep and slightly wider than the base stones. Check with your local building department to see if any restrictions apply. Pour a 6-inch gravel bed and tamp it.

■ Start by sorting out potential bonding stones. Broad or long enough to span the base of the wall, these bonding stones are set for stability at each end of the wall, and at least every 6 feet along its length.

■ Lay in the bottom course with the largest stones, angling them to tilt slightly toward the center of the wall. Build from both ends towards the center, with the stones' flattest sides up and the best sides out.

■ Set each stone carefully. If a stone doesn't fit well in one place, try it in another spot or set it aside for use later. Don't settle for an approximate fit. For staggered joints, set the stones to overlap each other like bricks in a running bond pattern.

■ Fill the gaps in the center of the wall with small stones so that the larger stones stay on the exterior and are securely in place.

■ Because only gravity and friction hold the stones in place, you'll have to slope (batter) the faces of the wall. Set back each course about 2 inches for every vertical foot.

To set the first (base) course of stones at or just below ground level, dig a shallow trench. Add a layer of gravel in the trench to make a stable base.

Bonding stones

The base course of stones should fit together neatly along the sides. Each additional course will depend on the stability of the base course. Set bonding stones that run from front to back every 6 feet or so to increase overall strength.

Build a slope or batter gauge to help keep the angle right. Nail a 2-foot 1×4 to a 4-foot 1×4 to form an "L." Tilt the longer board past 90 degrees—that's the angle of the set back. Nail a brace between the boards to hold them at that angle.

■ Install a drainage pipe in a gravel bed at the lowest surface of the wall.

MORTARED WALLS

A mortared wall requires a footing to support it and keep the mortared joints from cracking as the ground temperature changes. Check with your building department for local depth requirements. The footing will need to be dug below the frost line.

CONCRETE FOOTING: Dig a footing trench as thick as the wall and twice as wide. Make concrete forms of 2× lumber, set them in the trench, attached to 2×4 stakes. Drive the stakes into the ground, making sure the top of the forms are level.

■ Add a 4-inch layer of gravel to the bottom of the form. For large areas or in regions with severe winters, also use metal rebar or reinforcing wire mesh set on dobie blocks.

■ Pour concrete in the form, and level it with a screed board. You don't need to finish the surface as carefully as you would for a walkway, but it should be smooth and even.

MORTAR: Buy prepared dry mortar mix, or make it yourself from 1 part hydrated lime, 2 parts portland cement, and 9 parts washed construction sand. Add just enough water so the mixture stays together when you squeeze it into a ball.

■ Keep the mortar away from the outside faces as you place the stones. Lime will stain the stones.

CONSTRUCTION: Apply a bed of mortar 2 inches thick to the concrete footing. Set the first course from the ends to the middle.

■ Add mortar to all the joints between the stones, and fill the gaps in the center of the wall with small stones or gravel. Seal the joints well to prevent water from collecting inside the wall and weakening the mortar.

■ After the first course has set up, use a mason's trowel to add a layer of mortar to the top of the first course of stones. Then place the second course. Remember that mortar is not as strong as stone; even with it, the stones should still fit together closely.

■ Set bonding stones every 6 feet.

■ Set large, flat stones as the top course; add smaller stones under them until they are level. Fill the remaining joints with mortar.

CURING: Shade the wall and cover it with plastic sheeting to keep it damp and cool. For the best results, let it cure this way for a week.

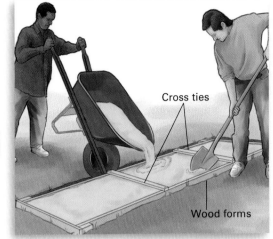

Cross ties

Wood forms

To build a mortared wall, use the strength and flat surface of a concrete footing. To keep the forms from losing their shape, set stakes around the edge, or add cross ties.

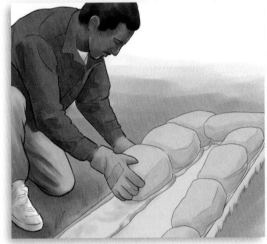

Spread mortar on the footing and set in the base course, fitting the stones as exactly as possible to the other's contours. Fill in with smaller stones. Let each course set before putting in the next one.

Finish the mortared joints with a joint striking tool for a neater appearance and to funnel water down the surface of the wall. Keep wet mortar off the faces of the stones to avoid a difficult cleanup job.

ROME WASN'T, EITHER

If your mortared stone wall has more than three courses—and most do—don't expect to build it in one day. Mortar needs time to harden before it can bear the weight of additional stones. Give yourself a rest and let time do some of the work.

RETAINING WALLS

Dry-stacked stone walls have been used as decorative borders for centuries. They also can make attractive retaining walls, but should be no higher than a few feet.

A well-built retaining wall will turn an unusable area into an outdoor living space, especially if the patio site is restricted by—or set at the bottom of—a slope. Sloped ground can restrict the size of the patio and cause increased runoff on the surface. If a retaining wall is an integrated part of the patio design, you'll need to excavate for it as part of the patio excavation and foundation work.

Plan and build your wall with care—it must restrain the soil (and water) behind it, and if it's not properly supported, it will collapse.

SUPPORT

You'll need a concrete footing reinforced with rebar and 10×10 reinforcing wire to support a mortared brick or stone wall. The footing should be as thick as the wall is wide, and twice its width. Footings for concrete walls are poured into forms when the wall is poured. Dry-set walls won't need a footing, but do require a 6-inch tamped gravel base for support and drainage. Set timber walls directly in a trench in the soil—no footing required.

Batter the front surface of dry stacked stone and timber walls—each succeeding course set back 2 inches for every foot of height. Build brick and poured concrete retaining walls with the faces set plumb and vertical.

MATERIALS

■ **WOOD FENCE WALLS:** Place pressure-treated 4×4 posts in footing holes at either end and at 4-foot intervals. Fill the holes with concrete and span the posts with pressure-treated 2× stock.

■ **CONCRETE BLOCK:** Mortar concrete blocks on a reinforced concrete footing, using ½-inch rebar set vertically in the footing and extending upward in the cells of the block. Fill the cells with concrete.

■ **TIMBERS:** Dig a trench wide enough to hold railroad ties or pressure-treated landscape timber (.40-grade and rated for ground contact). Stagger the joints for strength. Drill holes at regular intervals, and drive spikes or re-rod through the holes and into the ground.

■ **PRECAST CONCRETE BLOCK:** Dry-set interlocking block made specifically for walls or dry-set stone.

■ **BRICK OR RIVER STONE:** Mortar brick or stone to a concrete footing.

DRAINAGE

Retaining walls will buckle if the water in the soil doesn't have anywhere to go. Here's how to build a drainage system.

Dig a space between the wall and the unexcavated soil and lay in gravel and perforated drain pipe, sloping it 1 inch for every 4 feet. Fill the space with gravel, cover it with landscape fabric, then with soil and sod. The drainpipe must empty into a storm drain or a catch basin. If the wall is dry-stacked stone or timber, the spaces between the materials will act as "weep holes" that let the water pass through. You can also drill 1-inch holes every 2 feet in the second course of a timber wall.

Some concrete blocks are self battering—made with a ridge along the lower back edge that hooks against the block below and sets each course back from the one below. These interlocking blocks work best for walls that are no more than a few feet tall.

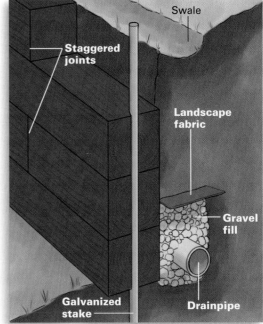

Pressure-treated timbers make an attractive retaining wall. To help prevent rot, install a drain pipe below and behind the wall and a swale (shallow trench) on top. Drive stakes through holes drilled in the timbers and into the ground.

A dry-stacked stone wall can take a long time to build; each stone must be fitted carefully for the wall to have any strength. Use dry-stacked stone for low walls only.

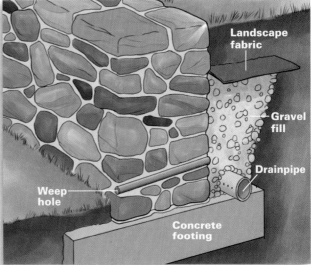

Mortared stone is the most permanent material to use for a retaining wall. Pour a concrete footing as the base. A large drainpipe carries away most rain water, and small drainpipes— called weep holes—let excess water through from the other side of the wall.

LIGHTING

Low-voltage lights are available in styles that range from Victorian revival to high-tech. Most are designed for use in the ground; many also can be mounted on deck railings, under stairs, or along fences. Halogen bulbs cost more initially, but they are less expensive to operate.

Lighting extends the use of your patio into the evening hours and makes your patio safer and more secure at night—even when you're not using it.

Adding lights to a patio takes planning and care, but it's not difficult. Choose the lighting system you prefer, review the installation guidelines, and prepare to enjoy your outdoor living area any time of day or night.

LINE VOLTAGE AND LOW VOLTAGE:

Lighting systems are either line voltage—the same 120-volt AC power as in your house—or low voltage, reduced by a transformer to 12 volts of direct current. Working with line voltage is easy enough for homeowners with experience doing their own electrical work. But it can be dangerous to use outdoors; you may want to hire professional electricians.

■ Most outdoor line-voltage wiring requires approval from a building inspector. Because low-voltage systems are safer for outdoor use, they seldom require inspection unless you add a new circuit. Always use care with electrical work, and follow all manufacturer's instructions carefully.

■ Each system has advantages. Low voltage is safe, easy to install, and inexpensive to operate. Line voltage is compatible with the wiring you already have, and it's useful for

outdoor appliances and power tools, as well as lighting. If you can't decide which system to use, think about which one matches your needs best.

CHOICES

■ A line-voltage system requires conduit, fittings, junction boxes, receptacles, fixtures, bulbs, wire, and connectors that meet building code requirements. Your supplier can tell you what other materials, tools, and hardware you'll need. Low-voltage systems are designed for use outdoors, and require fewer safety precautions for installation.

■ Several kinds of lights are available for both systems, but low-voltage systems generally offer more options. You can find lights to illuminate patio surfaces, walkways, and stairways. Others are made to show off plantings, walls, fountains, and other special features. Fixtures are available in a wide variety of materials—from molded plastic to hand-finished teak to cast bronze. The choices may surprise you.

■ A retailer who handles outdoor lighting may offer free design advice to customers. Take your plan along if you think you may need to ask for help.

INSTALLATION

LAYOUT: Using wooden stakes, mark where you plan to have lights, switches, junction boxes, and receptacles. Tie colored lines between the stakes to show where to dig trenches for wiring. Run the line to the power source.

■ Low-voltage systems may have limits on wire length. To keep wires shorter, place the transformer in a central location and run wires out to each fixture. If you need to run wire farther, call the manufacturer for advice.

CONDUIT: Cut away the sod where the trenches will go. Cut conduit to length and lay sections in place. Attach fittings as you work. Avoid making sharp bends in the conduit. The wire should be able to slide through it smoothly. Wherever the conduit will attach to a junction box or fixture, mount the junction box securely—to the side of the house, for example. Attach fittings to the conduit.

■ To run conduit under a walkway, dig on both sides of the path and drive an iron pipe through the ground with a sledge hammer. Push conduit through the hole as you pull the pipe out from the other side. While some low-voltage wiring can run above the ground, burying it is safer and neater. A shallow trench lined with plastic will protect the wiring and the appearance of your property.

WIRING: Using an electrician's tool called a fish tape, pull wire through the conduit to each junction box and receptacle. Pull out several inches of wire at each location for making the connections.

■ Run wire from the beginning of the circuit—or from the transformer of a low-voltage system—to the house wiring. Leave it unconnected for now.

■ If you're uncomfortable finishing the wiring yourself, have a professional electrician complete the job. Otherwise, wire the switches first, followed by the junction boxes, receptacles, and fixtures.

■ Make sure all outdoor circuits have ground fault interrupt (GFI) protection, and use waterproof gaskets on all exposed components. Point the open ends of all wire nuts downward so they don't collect water.

FINAL CONNECTIONS: Turn off the power at the main service panel. With all other parts of the system wired, connect it to the circuit you have chosen. Connect the parts of a low-voltage system to the transformer, and then plug it in. Check each connection to be sure everything is finished. Then turn the power back on.

■ Turn on each fixture to test the bulbs, and replace the ones that don't work. If any fixtures are not getting power, turn off the electricity at the main service panel and check the fixtures with a multitester. When all the fixtures work, adjust the lights at night to create the look you want.

CLEANING UP: When you are satisfied with the placement of your outdoor lighting, fill in the trenches and cover them with sod. Secure conduit and wires that extend above the ground. Now you're ready to enjoy an evening on your newly lighted patio.

If you need to run wire through areas that receive heavy foot traffic, bury the wiring in conduit for safety and convenience. Dig a trench to the depth specified by local codes, and join runs of conduit only with connectors designed for underground use.

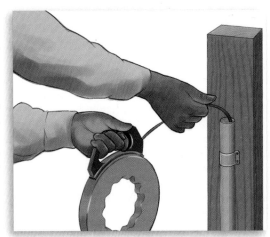

When the conduit is in place, you may have trouble pushing wire through it. To work around bends and over long distances, use a fish tape and pulling lubricant.

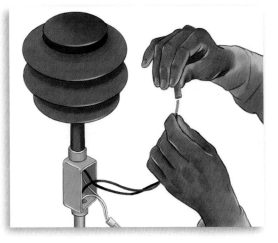

Tie the fixtures to the electrical supply lines with approved wire connectors. Turn on the power at the source to test the bulbs.

CARING FOR AN OLDER PATIO

Even the best laid patio surfaces will, from time to time, need some tender loving care. Proper maintenance, carried out regularly, will add years to your patio and to your enjoyment of it.

Don't rip out an old patio just because it shows some wear. If it's solid and its surface is in relatively good shape—and you like its location—it may be worth saving.

A few broken bricks or concrete chips aren't fatal flaws in the lives of patios—unless you're just itching to build a new one. Bear in mind that tearing out an old patio is hard work, so take a close look before you get out the sledgehammer. Those first few swings might be rollicking good fun, but it's amazing how quickly a sledge gains weight.

EVALUATING YOUR OLD PATIO

Start your inventory of patio conditions by looking for large cracks and sagging sections. These are good indicators the base is not adequate.

Dig down along the perimeter; you're looking for a 4-inch gravel base and 4 inches of concrete (for a slab or mortared patio) or a 4-inch gravel base and 2 inches of sand (for dry-set surfaces). If it's there, check the surface. It should be sloped for drainage—at least 1 inch for every 4 feet, and if you're going to mortar brick, tile, or stone on top, it should not contain any high spots more than ⅛-inch in 10 feet. If the surface is crowned in the center for drainage, that's okay for mortaring—as long as the crowning is gradual. Minor holes or flaking can be repaired. So can loose or damaged dry-set brick and tile. If the base is inadequate, it's time to pull it out.

DRY-SET MAINTENANCE

Dry-set brick and flagstone generally wear well and don't require much attention. If the edging and base have been properly installed and maintained, your routine chores will consist of an occasional weeding and replacement of the sand. (*To refill the joints, follow the sand-sweeping instructions on pages 62 and 81*). Beyond that, you may have to periodically remove moss or algae, or replace a heaved or damaged brick.

REMOVING MOSS AND ALGAE: Make a cleaning solution of an ounce of laundry soap, 3 ounces trisodium phosphate (or a nonphosphate TSP substitute), 1 quart chlorine bleach, and 3 quarts water. Brush it on, leave it for five minutes, then rinse.

Most grease and oil stains will come out with a little scrubbing with laundry detergent and warm water.

Stains that have penetrated need a more thorough treatment. Saturate the stain with mineral spirits and cover it with dry portland cement or cat litter. Let it stand overnight and sweep it away.

For more stubborn stains, try a paste of benzol and cat litter or cement. Let it stand for an hour and repeat if necessary.

Use these solutions to clean concrete, too.

REPLACING BRICK OR STONE: Pry up a heaved brick or flagstone with a sturdy crowbar (even a sand-set brick is unlikely to come out at the urging of a mere screwdriver).

Moisten the sand and reset the unit, tapping it with a rubber mallet. If it's still high, scrape a little sand out and reset it.

If you can't get a damaged piece out with a crowbar, break it up with a cold chisel (drive it with a baby sledge—pavers are hard). Then moisten and tamp the sand (use a 2×4) and set in new brick or stone. Sand-fill the joints as you would for a new patio.

ENLARGING PATIOS: Expansion generally amounts to a new patio area adjacent to the original. Refer to earlier sections in this book for specific information. You shouldn't have to worry much about the old materials falling into the new site while you're digging—if the gravel base was set correctly, it shouldn't move. And a wayward brick or two can be set aside and repositioned later.

CONCRETE CARE

Even the toughest of materials need a little tender care now and then.

ROUTINE CLEANING: Wash concrete occasionally with laundry soap and water.

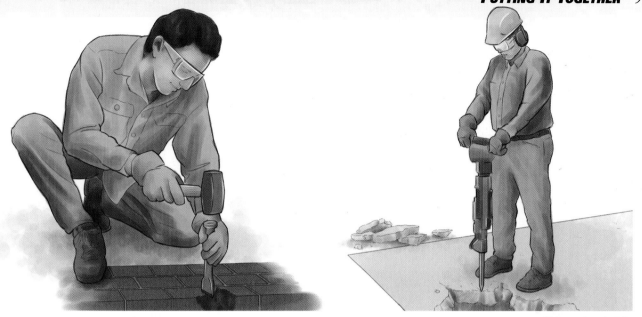

Chip out a brick (above left) using a baby sledge and a cold chisel.

Removing a concrete slab (above right) may call for the power of a rental jackhammer. Protect your eyes whenever you repair mortared surfaces.

STAINS: Scrub with a stiff broom or brush (don't use wire bristles on smooth concrete—the metal will mark the surface). Use muriatic acid to etch away stains that won't yield to standard cleaners. Mix 1 part acid to 9 parts water. Wear rubber gloves, old clothes, and eye protection—the acid is highly caustic. Scrub the mixture into the area with a stiff brush and let it stand for 10 minutes. Rinse.

REPAIR: Concrete surfaces suffer from several routine maladies:
- **DUSTING**: the surface wears away easily.
- **SCALING**: the surface flakes.
- **SPALLING**: deeper scaling.
- **CRAZING**: a network of surface cracks.
- **POP OUTS**: small holes.

You can deal with each of these problems fairly simply: Clean the area. Apply a latex bonding agent. Then trowel on a thin layer of concrete patch (a mix of portland cement, vinyl, and sand), feathering its edges.

Here's a better solution for all these problems, however, which also will work for cracks wider than ⅛ inch:
- Break out the affected surface with a small sledge and cold chisel to a depth of ½ to ¾ inch.
- Holding the chisel at an angle, "key" the outside edge of the area to be repaired—make it bigger on the bottom than the top. Keying a repair helps lock the patch in place.
- Remove all dust and concrete particles (a shop vacuum will do this quickly).
- Wet the surface with a latex concrete bonding agent and trowel on a layer of concrete patch.
- Smooth the surface with a steel trowel and texture it to match the surrounding area.

RESURFACING: If the surface damage is extensive but the slab is structurally sound, resurface it. Break up the damaged area or roughen it with a rented scarifier or sandblaster (both good candidates for a contractor). Build forms to accommodate the new height (you'll want to pour at least an inch of new surface). Apply latex bonding agent and pour the top coat.

DEMOLITION

Sometimes you have to get tough. If you have some masonry that just isn't making the cut, it won't leave gracefully.

CONCRETE SLAB: With or without a mortared surface, breaking up concrete is heavy work. You will need at least a 10-pound sledge—heavier is better, if you can handle it—and crowbars.
- Start at a corner and crack small sections. Pry out the section with a crowbar (pry against the unbroken surface, not against the surrounding soil) and carry it off in a wheelbarrow.
- Work your way across the surface, cracking and prying. The crowbar should do most of the work—concrete pries up more easily than you can pound it down.

If the slab is thicker than 4 inches, or you have a large area to remove, rent a masonry saw or jackhammer to make the job easier.

If in doubt, rent the equipment. There are no small jobs in demolition. Nobody will blame you if you for renting a jackhammer for a small area. And big power tools at least make an adventure of it. Save your strength for toting away all that broken-up concrete.
- Keep yourself safe—heavy gloves, steel toed-boots, and safety goggles are a must.

DRY-SET SURFACES: As adversaries go, these surrender more readily. To remove dry-set brick or flagstone, pry up a corner and remove each piece. Set them aside if they're not damaged; use them on your new surface.

GLOSSARY

3-4-5 METHOD: A technique for checking whether a corner is square. Mark a point 3 feet from the corner along one side; mark a point 4 feet from the corner along the other side. When the diagonal distance between the marks is 5 feet, the corner is square.

AGGREGATE: Gravel or crushed rock, mixed with sand, portland cement, and water to form concrete.

AWL: A sharp-pointed tool used for starting small holes for screws or for scribing lines.

BACKFILL: Soil used to fill in an excavation next to a wall; adds stability to the wall and keeps water away.

BASE: A prepared surface of gravel or sand that will support bricks, pavers, or concrete.

BATTER BOARD: A board frame supported by stakes set back from the corners of a structure.

BOND: A pattern in which masonry units, such as bricks, are arranged.

BRICK GRADE: The rating of a brick's durability, such as severe-weather (SW) and moderate weather (MW).

BRICKSET: A wide-bladed chisel used for cutting bricks and concrete blocks.

BUILDING CODES: Local rules governing the way structures may be built or modified.

BUTT JOINT: A joint formed by two pieces of material fastened end to end, end to face, or end to edge.

BUTTER: To apply mortar on bricks or blocks with a trowel before laying them.

CARPENTER'S LEVEL: A tool for establishing level over short distances.

CATCH BASIN: A hole for collecting water; often connected to a drain pipe.

CEMENT: A powder that serves as the binding element in concrete and mortar.

COMMON BRICK: Brick intended for general-purpose building; can be used for patio paving in milder climates.

CONCRETE: A building material made by mixing water with sand, gravel, and cement.

CONTROL JOINT: A groove tooled into a concrete slab during finishing to prevent uncontrolled cracking later on.

COURSE: A row of masonry units, such as bricks or stones.

CRUSHED STONE: Quarried rock that has been mechanically crushed and then graded so that most of the stones are of a similar size, but with varying shapes and colors.

CUBES OR BANDS: Pre-grouped quantities of pavers that will cover 16 lineal feet.

DARBY: A long-bladed float used to smooth large surfaces of freshly poured concrete.

DIMENSION LUMBER: A piece of lumber that is 2 inches thick and at least 2 inches wide.

DRAINAGE TRENCH: A shallow excavation for carrying water away from higher ground.

DRY-STACKED WALL: A wall of masonry units (stones) laid without mortar.

DRY WELL: A hole connected to the patio site by a drainpipe.

EDGER: A tool for rounding and smoothing concrete edges to finish and strengthen them.

EDGING: A border used to contain and define a surface; common materials are brick, concrete, plastic, and wood.

EXPOSED AGGREGATE: A concrete finish achieved by embedding rock into the surface.

FINISHING: The final smoothing stage in concrete work.

FLAGSTONE: Irregular shapes of flat natural stone, such as granite, bluestone, redstone, sandstone, limestone, and slate.

FLOAT: A rectangular wood or metal tool used to smooth and compress wet concrete.

FLUSH: On the same plane as, or level with, the surrounding surface.

FOOTING: A small foundation, usually made of concrete, used to support a post.

FROST HEAVE: An upward movement of soil caused when moist soil freezes.

FROST LINE: The maximum depth frost normally penetrates the soil.

GROUT: A thin mortar mixture used to fill the joints between tiles.

HAND DRILL: A small sledge hammer; used for breaking flagstones and driving larger chisels, such as bricksets.

JOINTER: A tool used for making control joints, or grooves, in concrete surfaces to control cracking.

LANDSCAPE FABRIC: Tightly woven fabric that allows water to flow through, but prevents weeds from growing up.

LAP JOINT: The joint formed when one member overlaps another.

LEVEL: The condition that exists when any type of surface is at true horizontal.

MASONRY CEMENT: A mix of portland cement and hydrated lime for preparing mortar.

MASON'S HAMMER: A tempered-steel hammer with a square face and a chisel-shaped claw.

MITER JOINT: The joint formed when two members meet that have been cut at the same angle, usually 45 degrees.

MORTAR: A mixture of masonry cement, masonry sand, and water; most often 1 part cement to 3 parts sand.

NOMINAL DIMENSIONS: The actual dimensions of a masonry unit, plus the thickness of the mortar joints on one end and at the top or bottom.

PAVERS: Cast concrete blocks, often dyed and shaped to fit in interlocking patterns.

PAVING BRICK: Brick of dense clay, fired to high temperatures to be hard and durable.

PLAN DRAWING: An overhead view of a structure, which shows locations of footings and framing members.

PLUMB: The condition that exists when a surface is at true vertical.

PLUMB BOB: A tool used to align points vertically.

POST: A vertical framing piece, usually 4×4 or 6×6, used to support a beam or a joist.

PREMIX: Any of several packaged mixtures of ingredients for preparing concrete or mortar.

PRESSURE-TREATED WOOD: Lumber or plywood soaked in a solution to make the wood resistant to water.

READY-MIX: Concrete that is mixed in a truck as it is being transported to the job site.

REBAR (REINFORCING ROD): Steel rod used to reinforce concrete and masonry structures.

REINFORCING WIRE MESH: A steel screening used to reinforce large areas of concrete.

RETAINING WALL: A wall constructed to hold soil in place.

RIVER ROCK: Medium-sized stones that have been smoothed by river or lake water.

RUBBLE: Uncut stone, often used for dry-stacked walls.

SCRATCH COAT: The first coat of mortar or plaster, roughened (scratched) so the next coat will stick to it.

SCREED: A straight edge used to level concrete as it is poured into a form or to level the sand base in a form.

SET: The process during which mortar or concrete hardens.

SETBACK: The minimum distance between a property line and any structure, as defined by local building codes.

SITE PLAN: A map showing the location of a new building project on a piece of property.

SPACER BLOCKS: Small blocks, also called dobie blocks, used to support reinforcing wire mesh for pouring concrete.

SQUARE: The condition that exists when one surface is at a 90-degree angle to another.

STRIKING: The process of finishing a mortar joint.

SUB-BASE: Soil or gravel, compacted to hold a base surface of gravel or sand.

TAMPER: A tool for compacting soil, gravel, sand, or other loose materials.

TROWEL: A flat and oblong or flat and pointed metal tool used for handling or finishing concrete and mortar.

WATER LEVEL: A tool for establishing level over long distances or irregular surfaces.

WEEP HOLE: An opening made in a mortar joint to allow water to drain through.

YARD: A unit of volume in which ready-mix concrete is sold; equal to a square yard (27 cubic feet).

This delightfully whimsical creation is successful by any definition. Its bold mix of tile, brick, and concrete took daring as well as extra time. But it continues to reward the homeowners day after day.

INDEX

METRIC CONVERSIONS

U.S. Units to Metric Equivalents			Metric Units to U.S. Equivalents		
To Convert From	Multiply By	To Get	To Convert From	Multiply By	To Get
Inches	25.4	Millimeters	Millimeters	0.0394	Inches
Inches	2.54	Centimeters	Centimeters	0.3937	Inches
Feet	30.48	Centimeters	Centimeters	0.0328	Feet
Feet	0.3048	Meters	Meters	3.2808	Feet
Yards	0.9144	Meters	Meters	1.0936	Yards
Square inches	6.4516	Square centimeters	Square centimeters	0.1550	Square inches
Square feet	0.0929	Square meters	Square meters	10.764	Square feet
Square yards	0.8361	Square meters	Square meters	1.1960	Square yards
Acres	0.4047	Hectares	Hectares	2.4711	Acres
Cubic inches	16.387	Cubic centimeters	Cubic centimeters	0.0610	Cubic inches
Cubic feet	0.0283	Cubic meters	Cubic meters	35.315	Cubic feet
Cubic feet	28.316	Liters	Liters	0.0353	Cubic feet
Cubic yards	0.7646	Cubic meters	Cubic meters	1.308	Cubic yards
Cubic yards	764.55	Liters	Liters	0.0013	Cubic yards

To convert from degrees Fahrenheit (F) to degrees Celsius (C), first subtract 32, then multiply by $\frac{5}{9}$.

To convert from degrees Celsius to degrees Fahrenheit, multiply by $\frac{9}{5}$, then add 32.